SKI
CANADA

WHERE TO SKI & SNOWBOARD

PATRICK TWOMEY

TRAILBLAZER PUBLICATIONS

Ski Canada – Where to ski & snowboard
First edition 1999

Publisher
Trailblazer Publications
The Old Manse, Tower Rd, Hindhead, Surrey, GU26 6SU, UK
Fax (+44) 01428-607571
trailblazer@compuserve.com
www.trailblazer-guides.com

British Library Cataloguing in Publication Data
A catalogue record for this book is available from the British Library

ISBN 1-873756-22-4

© Patrick Twomey 1999

The right of Patrick Twomey to be identified as the author of this work has been asserted by him
in accordance with the Copyright, Designs and Patents Act 1988

Photograph and map credits as follows:
Cover photo: © Jess Stock - Stock Shot; **Maps:** © Grouse Mountain; © Cypress Bowl; © Mount Seymour;
© Hemlock Valley Resort; © Manning Park; © Whistler/Blackcomb; © Mt Washington; © Sun Peaks
Resort; © Silver Star Mountain; © Big White Ski Resort; © Apex Mountain Resort; © Red Mountain;
© Whitewater Ski & Winter Resort; © Ski Whitetooth; © Ski Panorama; © Kimberley; © Fernie Alpine
Resort; © Wintergreen Ski & Golf Resort; © Ski Banff Mount Norquay; © Sunshine Village;
© Lake Louise; © Ski Marmot Basin; © Ski & Ride Kananaskis Country; © Castle Mountain Resort;
© Tremblant; © Mont Blanc; © Mont Saint-Saveur; © Le Relais Centre du Ski; © Ski Stoneham;
© Mont-Sainte-Anne; © Le Massif; © Ski Bromont; © Orford La Montagne; © Mont Sutton.

Editor: Anna Jacomb-Hood
Series Editor: Patricia Major
Typesetting: Anna Jacomb-Hood
Index: Jane Thomas

Every effort has been made by the author and publisher to ensure that the
information contained herein is as accurate and up to date as possible. However, they are unable to accept
responsibility for any inconvenience, loss or injury sustained by anyone as a result of the advice and
information given in this guide.

Printed by
Kelso Graphics (☎ 01573-223214), The Knowes, Kelso, TD5 7BH Scotland

SKI
CANADA
WHERE TO SKI & SNOWBOARD

PATRICK TWOMEY

TRAILBLAZER PUBLICATIONS

Patrick Twomey was born in western Canada and grew up skiing, cycling and climbing in the Rockies. Taking several years to complete university, he studied and lived in Calgary, Québec and Paris. After working at a variety of jobs, including digging potatoes in Ireland, he now takes North Americans on educational tours throughout Europe and leads British people through North America and further afield.

With a love of the outdoors and the natural beauty of his country, Patrick returns to his home in the Canadian Rockies as often as possible. While researching this guide he revisited much of Canada, putting thousands of kilometres on his car and spending weeks up in the mountains. He even managed to dislocate his shoulder on the slopes in Québec.

Acknowledgements

While this project did not always have the support of the weather, there are several people without whom I could not have completed it. The first thanks must go to Sarah Kerslake for her continuous support, help and great advice. My folks were also a wonderful help. My mom, Cathie gave up many hours going through the first draft, helping to find those phrases which made no sense at all.

Many others were instrumental along the way, particularly the folks at Silver Star and Mont-Sainte-Anne. Thanks to numerous resorts and tourist bureaux for the extended faxes during the postal strike. The Québec Tourist Office was particularly helpful.

My brother, Graham, and his roommates, Nicholas and Ted, were very entertaining hosts in Vancouver although I had to leave to get much writing done! Thanks also to Tom and Peg Volkers, Sue and Peter Rollison and Marian and Bernie Schor.

Rod Falkner, who is good fun to watch on a snowboard, was very helpful with the maps and all computer related questions. Tracy and Dave Harrington are not only great support but the best of skiing buddies.

Thanks to Pascal Wilson for providing lodging, a phone number and address in the UK. Many thanks also to Richard Polly of EF Tours and Jon Henley of Travelsphere for working around my dates.

Bryn Thomas at Trailblazer was the nucleus of this guide and helped me from start to finish. Thanks also to Allan MacDougall of Raincoast Books in Vancouver and to Anna Jacomb-Hood for editing the text.

A request

The author and publisher have tried to ensure this guide is as accurate and up-to-date as possible. However things change and ski conditions cannot be guaranteed. Prices rise, hotels open and close and resorts expand and change. Should you notice any omissions or changes that should be included in the next edition of this book, please write to Patrick Twomey at Trailblazer Publications (address on p2.) A free copy will be sent to persons making a significant contribution.

CONTENTS

INTRODUCTION

PART 1: PLANNING YOUR TRIP

PART 2: BRITISH COLUMBIA

PART 3: ALBERTA

PART 4: THE PRAIRIES

PART 5: ONTARIO

PART 6: QUEBEC

PART 7: ATLANTIC CANADA

GLOSSARY 165

INDEX 169

INTRODUCTION

Skiing is one of the most popular winter sports in Canada and with good reason. Exhilaration and challenge, combined with the awesome beauty of this northern land, give skiers one of the best ways to enjoy winter in the north. From the breathtaking beauty of the west to the historic cities of the east, Canada is perhaps most magnificent in winter.

A full quarter of Canadians ski or snowboard but few are aware of the diversity of alpine and nordic venues across their country. Of course most skiers have heard of Whistler and Banff, and Easterners are familiar with some of the larger resorts in Québec, but there are literally dozens of other areas worthy of serious attention. If you're interested in difficult terrain, great powder, cultural diversity, or just getting away from it all, there is a resort in Canada which fits your specific needs.

Over the years Canada has become a year-round destination and visitors from abroad are taking advantage of affordable prices and warm hospitality. More and more Canadian resorts offer first-class amenities and services for prices that remain very reasonable. If, however, you miss the good old days of slow lifts, empty runs and buckets of fresh powder you need only to head for the more remote areas of western Canada.

Canada's great resorts will likely continue to gain recognition for many reasons, in particular the variety of terrain they cover, their first-class restaurants and the nightlife on offer. But that quintessential winter experience – challenging runs and metres of powder – can, however, also be had at many lesser-known resorts that will doubtless never lose their basic appeal. The sport of alpine skiing itself is maturing and different ways of experiencing the winter slopes have now entered the mainstream. Snowboards are ever more common and many resorts have parks for snow-tubing, cross-country skiing and snowshoeing.

Along with great skiing and snow, Canada manages to maintain a rustic lack of pretension. Small ski communities are generally working class towns where you won't be judged on your appearance so much as your attitude. Excluding the famous world-class resorts, most destinations in Canada are still fairly undeveloped – just mountains for boarders and skiers, with maybe a couple of pubs and a hotel.

PART 1: PLANNING YOUR TRIP

As the world's second largest country, Canada's topography is far from consistent, providing almost all kinds of conditions imaginable. Skiing has developed here out of small, isolated communities and is regional by nature. Canadians living around major ski areas tend to be very faithful to their local resort and drive or take the appropriate shuttle on their day off. However, for those who live too far from good skiing to enjoy a day visit, or for the thousands of foreign visitors, a ski trip to Canada means travelling this mighty land during winter.

Canadian ski resorts are generally much less crowded than elsewhere in the world and lift lines are all but non-existent at the more remote mountains. The reality of visiting Canada during winter is that you will rarely stand in line for anything – unless the road needs to be cleared of an avalanche.

When to go

Based on national averages, Canada is the coldest country in the world and over 30% of its precipitation falls as snow – that percentage can be doubled in some mountain and inland regions, particularly the fairly dry Prairies. During the winter months the majority of Canadians have to cope with temperatures that are well below freezing and with the qualified exception of the south western coastal areas, most are surrounded by snow. The title 'The Great White North' has stuck for a reason.

It is very difficult to choose a best time to go as regions vary, as do seasons and prices. While many resorts open in November, full operation usually doesn't get under way until December. Lower elevation resorts and those exposed to the oceans can often remain closed until Christmas. Snow is generally reliable through March, but by April it is a good idea to check conditions. A few mountains, however, have been known to stay open until July!

The single most popular period for a ski vacation is over Christmas and the New Year when almost everyone has a few days off work or school, so from about December 20 to January 6 the slopes are crowded. The advantages of this time are the wonderful atmosphere – lights dot the landscape – and the fact that resorts often put on extra activities. Other popular periods are around Easter and in March when schools have their annual breaks. Generally students are given a week and many join ski groups. If the idea of sharing the slopes with young groups is unappealing just call ahead because the resorts are always given a fair amount of warning.

There are also regional considerations that can affect best times to go. Québec City, for instance, comes alive with its winter festival in early February, and Banff is much more affordable if you go well after the New Year. Daylight is an issue in late December, particularly further north, although a full day of skiing is always possible throughout the season. By late February the sun shines well past 6pm in most southern regions and the days can be somewhat warmer.

TEMPERATURE
Average temperatures can vary significantly as does humidity, although generally the three Prairie provinces are the coldest. Skiers from the USA and Europe may

❏ **Average winter temperatures and snowfall for selected cities**
(Environment Canada)

	High	Low (°C)	Snowfall (cm)
Vancouver	5.7	0.1	55
Calgary	-3.6	-15.7	135
Edmonton	-8.7	-19.8	127
Winnipeg	-13.2	-23.6	115
Toronto	-2.5	-11.1	124
Montréal	-5.8	-14.9	214
Québec	-7.7	-17.3	337
Halifax	-1.5	-10.3	261

As city snowfall often bears little relationship to the conditions in nearby mountains, average snowfall for specific resorts is listed in the relevant section of this guide.

find temperatures in general colder than at home, but not uncomfortably so. Should you venture out in -30°C, however, you will find the snow superb and the trails uncrowded. Unfortunately the huge variations in relative humidity between coastal and continental regions make comparisons almost pointless. The extreme colds of the Prairies are fairly easy to handle with a good jacket and touque, whereas -20°C in Montréal is almost unbearable. Certain valleys have warmer average temperatures and faster lifts mean less time to cool off. The big decision is whether to brave slightly lower temperatures for consistent snow or wait for the warmth of spring but then also risk more varied conditions.

Getting there

GETTING TO CANADA

While ski slopes can be found in every Canadian province, the reality is that foreign visitors will likely make their way to one or more of the major resort centres and give the flatter regions a miss. The natural gateways for skiers are Vancouver, Calgary, Montréal and Québec. Ottawa and Edmonton are also ports of entry, although they are less convenient for ski destinations.

Skiing in Québec is appealing to East Coast Americans and Europeans as flight times are shorter and prices attractive. The largest gateway is **Montréal** since few international flights arrive into **Québec City**. Skiers in search of the big mountains should fly into either Vancouver or Calgary. Certainly the easier of the two is **Vancouver** as the airport is busy with an ever increasing number of flights. This is the ideal choice if you're just planning a one-week visit to Whistler or if you want to fly into the Okanagan. **Calgary** is a smaller, more friendly airport with regular flights from the UK, the USA and other Canadian cities. This is the principal gateway to the Rockies and Banff as well as to other major resorts such as Panorama (3^1/2 hours), Fernie (3^1/2 hours) and Jasper (4^1/2 hours). Jasper is about the same distance from **Edmonton**, though the Edmonton road is less likely to close.

If you are planning to visit several resorts during your holiday it is well worth taking distances into account as it's easy to under-estimate travel times in Canada. Toronto, for example, is a four-hour flight from the Rockies and an eight-hour drive from Montréal. Trying out different ski hills is fun, but fitting in too many over a short period can often be frustrating. Winter travel can be difficult and while highways are generally clear, access roads can be slow going.

❏ TOUR OPERATORS

Canada and USA
● Skiers planning a vacation at any of the resorts in this book are advised to book direct on the telephone numbers or Web sites given in each resort section of this guide. Alternatively bookings can be handled by your local travel agent.

UK
● **All Canada Travel & Holidays** (☎ 01502-585825, brochure ☎ 01502-5615176, fax 01502-500681, www.all-canada.com), Sunway House, Raglan Rd, Lowestoft, Suffolk NR32 2LW
● **Canada's Best** (☎ 01904-658436, fax 01904-634598, www.dialspace.dial.pipex.com/town/place/qr38), 170 Fulford Rd, York, North Yorkshire YO1 4DA
● **Canada Ski Club** (☎ 01727-841177, fax 01727-841418) 20 Heritage Close, High St, St Albans, Herts AL3 4EB
● **Canadian Connections** (☎ 01494-473173, fax 01494-473588, email: cdream1059@aol.com), 10 York Way, Lancaster Rd, High Wycombe, Bucks HP12 3PY
● **Crystal Holidays Ltd** (☎ 0181-399 5144, fax 0181-390 6378, www.crystalholidays.co.uk), Crystal House, Arlington Rd, Surbiton, Surrey KT6 6BW
● **Experience Canada** (☎ 01323-416699, fax 01323-410864, email: experience.hols@btinternet.com), 14 Terminus Rd, Eastbourne, East Sussex BN21 3LP
● **First Choice Ski** (☎ 0990-557755, fax 01273-676410), Olivier House, 18 Marine Parade, Brighton, East Sussex BN2 1TL
● **Frontier Ski** (☎ 0181-776 8709, fax 0181-778 0149, www.frontier-ski.co.uk), Broadmead House, 21 Panton St, London SW1Y 4DR
● **Inghams** (☎ 0181-780 4444, fax 0181-780 4405, www.inghams.co.uk), 10-18 Putney Hill, London SW15 6AX
● **Media Travel** (☎ 01784-434434, fax 01784-431415), Lawrence House, 45a High St, Egham, Surrey TW20 9DP
● **Ski Activity** (☎ 01738-840888, fax 01738-840079), Lawmuir House, Methven, Tayside PH1 3SZ
● **Ski Club of Great Britain** (☎ 0181-410 2000, fax 0181-410 2001, www.skiclub.co.uk), The White House, 57-63 Church Rd, Wimbledon, London SW19 5SB
● **Ski Independence (Osprey Holidays)** (☎ 0990-550555, fax 0990-502020, www.ski-independence.co.uk), Broughton Market, Edinburgh, Lothian EH3 6NU
● **Ski the American Dream** (☎ 0181-552 1201, fax 0181-552 7726, www.skidream.com), 1-7 Station Chambers, High St North, London E6 1JE
● **Ski Connections** (☎ 01494-473173, fax 01494-473588, email: amcon@httrav.co.uk), 10 York Way, Lancaster Rd, High Wycombe, Bucks HP12 3PY
● **SkiSar US** (☎ 01959-575727, fax 01959-540797), Fairhand Holidays, Suite 5, 216 Main Rd, Biggin Hill, Kent TN16 3BD

Australia
● **Ski Arama** (☎ 02-9580-6555, fax 02-9580-0157), 41 Dora St, Hurstville, 2220 NSW
● **Value Tours** (☎ 02-9262-2333, fax 02-9262-2780), Level 1, 350 Kent St, Sydney, 2001 NSW
● **Travel Plan** (☎ 02-9438-1333, fax 02-9906-5058), 72 Chandos St, St Leonards, 2065 NSW
● **Ski Max** (☎ 02-9267-1655, fax 02-9267-1644), Level 3, 263 Clarence St, Sydney, 2000 NSW
● **Alpine World** (☎ 02-9955-3744, fax 02-9955-3944), 343 Pacific Highway, Crows Nest, 2065 NSW

New Zealand
● **Ski Travel Specialists** (☎ 09-307-1350, email: atskitravel.co.nz), The Snow Centre, 71 Stanley St, Parnell, Auckland
● **Galaxy United Travel** (☎ 07-347-9444, fax 07-348-1844), 1316 Tutanexai St, Rotarua

Skiers from Europe, Australia and New Zealand will probably be amazed by the ever increasing number of Canadian ski packages available (see Tour Operators on p11). Many of these offers do represent great savings, however you will likely be restricted to one region and one hotel. This makes sense if you're planning a holiday in Whistler or Banff, where there are several mountains to visit, but could be limiting unless you already know you will enjoy an extended stay at a particular resort. Some operators are, however, now offering Ski Safaris, enabling you to visit more than one resort.

With the exception of the Christmas/New Year period, flights to Canada are generally less expensive during winter. Canada's two major airlines are Air Canada and Canadian Airlines International. British Airways, Qantas, Air New Zealand as well as all the major American airlines fly to different cities in Canada. Flying within Canada is also appealing to foreign visitors as winter road conditions are variable and flights are often cheaper when booked overseas.

Both of Canada's major airlines have larger international networks, which often means that students and people under 26 can find deals with bonus internal flights. It is also worth watching for different promotional North America air passes. Generally these offer fairly unrestricted travel on subsidiary airlines and must be purchased outside of Canada and by non-Canadian residents.

It is best to book flights several weeks in advance, although travellers from the UK can often find great last minute deals to North America. Charter packages can be quite restrictive, but are bringing costs down for flights between Canada and Australia, New Zealand and the UK. The choice is still fairly limited although return flights from New Zealand and Australia to Vancouver shouldn't cost more than $1500. February is probably the cheapest time to come and still enjoy great skiing. Flying to Calgary should not cost much more, however if you're going all the way to Québec expect to pay an extra $200-$300. When visiting both sides of North America 'Around the World' flights often prove just as reasonable.

From the UK your choice is more varied. Regular winter promotions mean flights to eastern Canada can come as low as £250. Good deals to Calgary and Vancouver will always cost above £400 once taxes are included.

Americans have a great selection of direct flights to Vancouver. Most flights to Calgary pass through Salt Lake City. If flying to Québec you will find many flights to Montréal but few to Québec City. Californians can often find flights to western Canada for under US$200 while Easterners will pay at least US$400 to fly to Vancouver. With the amount of business between New England and Québec, good flight deals can often be found. Generally flights within Canada are less expensive than those within the USA. The recent market problems in Asia have meant a decrease in visitors and consequently lower flight prices.

Americans driving north will find roads in good condition and considerably less crowded than at home. While gas is traditionally a little more expensive than in the USA, a weaker Canadian dollar equalises any difference. Seat belts are now the law everywhere in Canada and road signs are in kilometres, not miles. Your US driver's license is sufficient identification for crossing the border and it is well worth buying a bottle of your favourite booze at duty free as liquor tends to be much more expensive in Canada.

❑ **ID, passports and visas**
American citizens do not need visas or passports as long as they have good photo ID. Most Europeans along with Australians, New Zealanders and Japanese citizens do not need visas, but do require a passport (valid for at least six months).

GETTING TO THE RESORT

Travelling across Canada during the winter months cannot be taken lightly – no region of the country is unaffected. However you choose to travel to the resort, it is generally a good idea to have your trip worked out ahead of time. While visitors will certainly see locals hitching up to the hills, boards in hand, trying to cover too much distance in one day can be challenging. No one enjoys driving long distances after a day of skiing and the requisite après ski beer.

Many resorts offer local shuttle services although these are by no means universal. Local services are listed under the individual sections.

By plane

Air Canada (North America ☎ 1-888-247-2262, UK ☎ 0990-247726) and Canadian Airlines (North America ☎ 1-800-665-1177, UK ☎ 0345-616767), along with their subsidiaries, fly almost everywhere in Canada and most ski areas are within a reasonable distance of local airports. Flying can be somewhat less expensive during winter and, excluding the Christmas/New Year period, planes often have plenty of space. If, however, you plan on flying some of the smaller commuter routes away from major centres then it is reasonable to expect a few delays during winter.

Tickets from Toronto to western Canada that are purchased in advance generally cost between $300 and $400, while the full fare runs as high as $1500. Watch for specials which can bring tickets down to under $300. The cost of a flight from Montréal to Calgary or Vancouver is fairly similar and the $10 Dorval airport improvement tax is well worth the fee! Vancouver airport also has a $10 departure tax ($15 for international flights). Flights from other Canadian centres to the west and the east often involve changing planes in Toronto or Montréal.

Regional airports make the journey to some resorts even simpler. One of the most appealing is Kelowna's airport in the heart of the Okanagan, since it saves driving over mountain passes.

By car

Due to the nature of the country, Canadians are accustomed to the adventures of winter driving. Nonetheless, the number of road accidents rises every winter with black ice being the big killer on open highways. Skiers are certainly used to poor road conditions and while mountain access roads are slowly improving, getting to some of the west's more remote hills often involves climbing steep unpaved roads. Good winter tires are a must and chains are highly recommended (and required on more isolated routes and for Mt Washington on Vancouver Island). Access roads in the east are generally easier to manage, although the main highways can be hard to see with blowing snow.

Driving in The Kootenays often involves road closures due to snowfall, and Whitewater is approached by a fairly difficult 10km access road. Castle Mountain in Alberta is at the end of a quiet road which tends to accumulate ice, and the last few kilometres up to Apex near Penticton can be hair-raising. Whistler is easily accessible, as is Banff, although traffic is heavier in these areas. Le Massif, north east of Québec, involves a steep downhill on a fairly old road.

It takes a particularly heavy storm to slow down major routes and Canadian roads are well patrolled. Nonetheless it is always a good idea to carry blankets and candles and take note of road signs saying 'Next Gas 100km'. Animals are often a hazard in the mountains and there is no winner in a collision with an elk.

Car rental is fairly affordable and can be booked through your travel agent or directly with one of the rental companies. The smallest two-door vehicle can be rented for around $30 a day or $200 per week, however full insurance can cost as much as $20 a day extra. A fully-equipped four-wheel drive is closer to $500 per week. It is important to try and return your vehicle to the place it was rented from as drop-off penalties can be high.

International companies include: **Avis** (North America ☎ 1-800-879-2847, UK ☎ 0990-900500, www.avis.com), **Budget** (North America ☎ 1-800-267-0505, UK ☎ 0800-181181, www.budget.ca), **Hertz** (North America ☎ 1-800-263-0600, UK ☎ 0990-906090, www.hertz.com), and with less comfort but lower prices: **Rent a Wreck** (North America ☎ 1-800-327-0116).

Distances from resorts to main centres are outlined in individual sections. If your accommodation does not provide underground parking, you will need an extension cord to plug in your car engine heater at night.

By bus

Coach travel has generally been the preferred form of transportation for young people travelling around North America, however services are becoming more expensive. Watch out for flight deals which can be just as cheap in winter. The entire bus industry in Canada is presently going through changes with companies being bought out and new ones joining the market. For long distance travel, Greyhound remains the largest mover of people. Multi-week bus passes can be bought overseas and are sometimes available in Canada.

There are plenty of other inter-city services though they are less frequent during the winter. The main text covers shuttle services to and from different resorts where available.

Making a booking

Day skiers obviously don't need to worry about booking tickets, although it may be worth purchasing shuttle tickets in advance if travelling from a major centre. Most of the larger resorts in Canada have a central reservations number which makes booking easy. Simply call the resort and give them your time frame and price range and a response will be immediate. Bookings often require a 25% deposit with full payment one month before your arrival date. Late cancellations usually incur hefty penalties.

Space in condos is available throughout the season, although the Christmas and New Year period is often booked as much as a year in advance and resorts do not always accept short stays over this holiday period. Easter is also very busy as are long weekends. For lower prices and emptier runs visit midweek.

From the USA bookings do not need to be any more complicated as you can easily contact resorts directly or via your travel agent. The number of different companies offering packages to Canada is considerable and many provide good value, particularly when flights are included.

The tourist information numbers listed with each province are often toll free from the USA as are the numbers for the particular resorts. Web site home pages are included for resorts where available.

❑ **El Niño**
Perhaps the only occasions when it may not be worth buying a season pass are those years when an El Niño weather system forms in the Pacific. This peculiar change happens every few years and when it does it tends to cause havoc throughout the Pacific Rim. In light of the many storms resulting from El Niño, western Canada is fortunate, but the warm dry weather is not a dream come true for the ski resorts.

From further afield it is possible to organise your own trip with flights, cars and accommodation. However, many travel companies offer package ski deals which represent good value, particularly for Europeans. Do shop around, though.

Costs

Needless to say, skiers and boarders have chosen expensive sports. New equipment can easily cost hundreds of dollars and resorts are generally not geared to people on a tight budget. Those living close to resort areas should always consider a season pass or at least a discount card. As more and more resorts are combining their marketing, interchangeable passes are becoming common. Season passes and discount cards are almost always less expensive if bought before the season begins.

Lift ticket costs are fairly comparable to resorts in other countries, however ski packages are often less expensive than elsewhere and seem a downright bargain when compared to Switzerland and Austria. Food is cheaper than in Europe and gas is less than half price. Overall, costs have traditionally been slightly higher than in the United States but a weak Canadian dollar is a bonanza for Americans who are being drawn north by attractive prices. Hotels are almost always proportionally cheaper with two or more people and inclusive packages offer great savings.

It is important to choose your destination well if cost is an issue as there are surprising differences in overall prices. Whistler is very expensive in almost all ways imaginable, whereas some of the smaller resorts in British Columbia (BC) offer great deals. Differences between low and high season dramatically affect prices and everything is at its most expensive over Christmas and New Year. For those who don't worry too much about cost, Canada has some grand old hotels, and major resorts offer all the amenities imaginable. If you are a proficient skier and have some extra cash, Canada is home to some of the world's best heli-skiing (see p19). Prices are lower than in Europe, but you'll still need a few hundred dollars for a day's heli-skiing.

The budget skier who is happy staying in a youth hostel and packing a lunch can get by on around $80 per day. Couples who enjoy good accommodation and good food along with a nice hot lunch on the mountain should plan on $120-$150 per person per day. Lift ticket prices start at about $30 and top out around $55 per day for an adult, and there are usually reduced prices for children, teenagers, students and seniors. Passes for more than one-day's skiing almost always represent a saving. Staying in a condo is ideal for groups who want a place to stay that's convenient and good value; all resorts with on-hill accommodation have them.

TAXES
In the great North American tradition the price marked is not the price paid. **Prices quoted in this guide exclude sales tax.** All of Canada is subject to a 7% Goods and

---

❑ **Rates of exchange**
Americans will receive around CDN$1.40 for each US$1 and most resorts and some restaurants will accept US currency. Change will always be given in Canadian dollars.

The British are the big winners receiving around CDN$2.30 for every pound. Aussies receive a little less than CDN$1 for theirs and Kiwis will get around CDN$0.85.

Inflation in Canada is almost non-existent so prices in this guide will not change dramatically. If something costs a 'loonie' hand over a one dollar coin; a 'twoonie' is the two dollar version.

Services Tax (GST) and every province except Alberta has a Provincial Sales Tax (PST). This varies from province to province, but tops out at 12% in Newfoundland. Provinces also have their own hotel taxes. Visitors are eligible for a GST refund on all purchases being taken out of Canada and some provinces have a PST rebate. The provincial refund is available in Québec, but not BC. Keep all receipts and apply upon departure from Canada.

Accommodation

There is a rather consistent, or even generic, aspect to ski resort lodging in Canada. While appearances differ from resort to resort and region to region, one need only imagine fairly good, clean, North American rooms to have an idea of what their hotel or condo will be like inside.

The most popular form of accommodation is the **condominium**. Essentially condos sleep between four and 12 people and each is equipped with a kitchen, a bathroom, and often with a deck and a barbecue. No complex is complete without a hot tub and more expensive units have private ones. Almost every resort in Canada with on-hill accommodation will have condos. While prices vary, a rough guideline is $50 per person per night, based on four people sharing. Most condo complexes also have a small store and some even include a pub. Many condos are in fact privately owned and therefore the contents and upkeep can vary. Of course if you fall in love with a certain resort it is often possible to purchase a unit and have the local management company rent it out for some of the year.

Many resorts have **hotel accommodation**. Hotels tend to be equivalent in price to condos but do not offer self-catering facilities. Nonetheless they are clean, have maid service and often include underground parking. Most hotels have storage areas for equipment as they don't like skis marking walls. Hotels also always have restaurants and pubs along with cable TV and other amenities. It is rare to find a ski area hotel with less than a three-star rating.

Chalets can also be rented from private owners via a management company. If you have a large group this is the way to go as the cottages are usually well maintained and attractive. As is true with hotels and condos, prices decrease based on the length of walk from the nearest lift.

Après ski

With the exceptions of Whistler, Banff, Tremblant and some smaller ski towns such as Kimberley and the villages being built around the resorts in the Okanagan, evening activities are limited. The majority of resorts in the east and some in the west offer night skiing, and almost every resort in Canada has a lounge and a cafeteria at the base of the slopes, but little else. If you need some entertainment at the end of a day's skiing you'll probably find a band playing in the bar, or you may have to drive into the nearest town.

In Québec you are rarely far away from a city or an interesting community with a good choice of restaurants but small town western Canada generally comes with a couple of bars and a few basic places to eat. It is this relaxed, rustic feel which seems to attract so many skiers to Canada.

❑ **Open all hours?**
An ever-increasing number of Canadian resorts offer night skiing although many do not as yet have a market for it. Night skiing aside, it is time that some resorts woke up to the length of a day. Some, particularly in eastern Canada, do stay open right through to sunset, but there are others which religiously close the lifts down at 3.30 or 4pm. For the frequent, fit skier who has climbed the mountain at 10am after paying nearly $50 for a ticket, it seems a touch excessive to close everything down when the sun is still high and the snow soft. In fact by early March the light is often better by late afternoon.

Skiing with children

Alpine and cross-country skiing have always been ideal family sports and most resorts are very well equipped for children of all ages. Cross country is undoubtedly the much more affordable option as trail fees are either free or a fraction of the cost of alpine lift tickets. Equipment is also more affordable, although good clearance sales, or second-hand deals can significantly cut the cost for alpine gear.

Kids tend to prefer going downhill and they take to the sport quickly. They are usually more willing to challenge themselves and they're less likely to break a limb if they fall. Ski resorts see the value in starting people off young and are constantly expanding their 'kinderski' programs. You can expect to pay around $45 per day for your kids to be taken care of and taught to ski. Basic daycare goes for around $25 a day.

The downside to skiing with kids is the general lack of evening activities for them. For this reason it may be worth day-tripping from larger centres or heading to resorts such as Banff. Large resorts like Whistler have plenty of entertainment but become very expensive. Smaller destinations such as Silver Star near Vernon call themselves family resorts and cater to that market; thus they provide an extensive ski school, organised evening games and activities, but not a big drinking environment. The older resorts in Québec and some in Ontario have always been geared towards families who leave the big cities on weekends. Less developed resorts mean less structured entertainment but also lower prices. Out in the mountains and after a full day skiing kids rarely stay awake late into the evening anyway.

Learning to ski

Like all sports, skiing comes naturally to some and is a definite struggle for others. There certainly seems to be a correlation between fear and age. Most of the little tykes racing down the hills with helmets (now the law on Prince Edward Island) and no poles end up skiing for years. The other bonus for youngsters is that they seem to be less likely to suffer broken limbs than fully grown skiers.

All mountains offer ski instruction for varying costs and the Canadian Federation of Ski Instructors is a well organised and managed organization. It is a good idea to have a few lessons when you first take up the sport, and some people find it very helpful to take refresher courses every so often. Resorts now have instructors qualified to teach skiers of all levels.

❏ **What is a Black Run?**
There is an unfortunate inconsistency in the evaluation of run difficulty. While you may feel you have mastered the expert runs of one mountain, the next resort finds you side-slipping down. Certainly all major hills do their best to mark runs uniformly, however beginners who manage an advanced run off a small base lift should be cautious about heading for the summit. Double blacks are becoming more common although very few mountains claim or deserve to have triples. Some hills automatically designate treed or ungroomed runs as double black, whereas others reserve such designations for the truly extreme. Before riding expert-only chairs it is always worth gauging the general feel of a mountain.

Smaller resorts tend to upgrade runs in order to present a more diverse terrain, although certain larger resorts insist on exaggerating areas and being over generous in their run count. Regardless of how many names or numbers are allocated, a run is a run.

Snowboarding is popular with people who haven't grown up on snow as it is perhaps a little easier to master the basics. Lessons are also recommended as the basic boarding stance does not always come naturally. As snowboarders often ride in groups and much of the fun is in doing tricks, boarders often learn from each other and learn from falling.

Basic, introductory group lessons are offered at all resorts and generally cost around $25 for 1½ hours. Private lessons start at around $40, but are not worth the money if you're new to skiing because the basics can be learnt easily in a group. A great variety of programs exist for young skiers, and Canadian schools often offer instruction to their students. A new skier can certainly be in a position to enjoy a large part of the mountain after only a week's worth of lessons. Larger resorts offer inclusive packages with equipment rental included.

Skiers switching to boards can often get the hang of it with one lesson. The most important thing here is to learn where to put your weight. Boarding lessons are on average a few dollars more expensive, but even the first time rider will likely need fewer hours of instruction to grasp the basics.

Snowboarding

Undoubtedly the fastest growing alpine sport, Canadian resorts have now fully-embraced boards. Long past are the days of having to wear licenses and being restricted to certain runs. Most larger resorts have half-pipes and lessons are offered everywhere. The sport emerged from the skateboarding and surfing traditions and although boarders have a sub-culture of their own, the thrill of riding is in no way limited to any one group. The sport is still generally marketed towards younger people, although with its inception as an Olympic event and its popularity with latecomers to the mountains, it is destined to continue growing. As snowboarding gains recognition it will inevitably become more regulated. Many larger hills now have machines for cutting the perfect half-pipe and made-to-order snowboard parks are being constructed. Hopefully this won't cause traditionalists to move on to different sports. It was refreshing to watch the group of young boarders having a good time in the half-pipe during the Nagano Olympic Games, with not all the emphasis on winning.

While the scope for development of skills on a snowboard is just as great as with skis, boards do allow newcomers to the slopes a faster way to enjoy more of a mountain. Particularly for those who have not grown up on skis, snowboarding seems to be a little easier to pick up.

❏ **Heli-skiing**

Perhaps the greatest thrill for any advanced skier is to experience, at least once, the perfect powder and timeless silence at the top of an untouched mountain. Heli-skiing is the absolute upper end of the skiing industry and the only difficulty, aside from the truly prohibitive costs, is sharing a mountain after having one all to yourself.

British Columbia has by far the largest selection of operators and mountains. Some resorts offer the possibility of one-day heli trips, while other outfits have inclusive first-class packages. You're doing well if you find a one-day package for under $400 and a one-week inclusive for under $4000. Try the following:

Mountain Helisports (Whistler) ☎ 604-932-2070 or ☎ 1-888-HELISKI
Tyax Heli-Skiing (Whistler) ☎ 604-932-7007 or ☎ 1-888-435-4754
Whistler Heli-skiing ☎ 604-932-4105
Mike Wiegele Heli-Village Resort (Blue River) ☎ 250-673-8381 or ☎ 1-800-661-9170
Robson Helimagic Inc (Valemont) ☎ 250-566-9767
Great Canadian Heli-skiing (Golden) ☎ 250-344-2326
Kootney Helicopter Skiing (Nakusp) ☎ 250-265-3121 or ☎ 1-800-663-0100
RK Heli-Ski Panorama ☎ 250-342-3889 or ☎ 1-800-661-6060
Selkirk Tangiers Helicopter Skiing (Revelstoke) ☎ 250-344-5016 or ☎ 1-800-663-7080
Last Frontier (Vernon) ☎ 250-558-7980 or ☎ 1-888-655-5566
THL (Vernon) ☎ 250-558-5379 or ☎ 1-800-667-4854
CMH (Banff) ☎ 403-762-7100 or ☎ 1-800-661-0252

Perhaps as a result of the soft powder, or the more relaxed atmosphere, boarding is more common in the west. Skiers who live for powder should at least once enjoy the pleasure of floating effortlessly on a board. With the exception of snowboard parks, skiers and boarders can enjoy the same terrain. Snowboards, however, are somewhat more at the mercy of snow conditions as the wider base surface slides even more easily on ice, and the lack of poles makes flat ground a real drag.

As the sport grows and gains international recognition it becomes easy to imagine a day when there are as many riders as skiers.

Cross country and back country

Canada is a mecca for cross-country fans, and although Europeans still dominate the sport in competition, over one fifth of all Canadians cross-country ski. There is not a city in Canada without easy access to cross-country trails and with back-country skiing factored in, the options are almost limitless! Many resorts now have adjoining tracks and the overall costs are much lower. Obviously skiing away from a centre has some inherent risks and real adventurers should take appropriate avalanche precautions. Skiers who are thinking of exploring back-country routes are well advised to purchase a book on mountain survival or even take one of the many courses offered. Universities are a good place to inquire.

If you plan on exploring trails that involve open snow faces or camping, it is essential you do not go alone or even with someone equally inexperienced. Avalanche beacons which make finding you much easier are now available and should always be carried. Park information centres provide updated avalanche information and you are required to register before setting out on a major journey.

Equipment is also important as is clothing – regardless of how cold a day it is a serious cross-country skier will work up a sweat. Back-country skiers are recommended to carry a spare ski tip as nothing is more unpleasant than trekking out of the mountains on one ski! Recreational cross-country skiers may be attracted by wax-less skis which are slow and make climbing hills easier, however they soon prove frustrating and limiting. You also have to make a decision between classic and skating styles. Essentially classic allows you to explore and go at your own pace whereas skating is the racer's form of the sport.

Equipment

The variety of equipment options is enormous as too are the potential costs. The good news is that you do not need to dress up to ski in most places in Canada. It makes more sense to buy good gear and the skis or board that is right for you.

SKIS AND BOARDS

Advances in bindings have made them much safer and a new set is well worth the money. Skis are becoming more job specific so it is worth considering what sort of style you prefer. Skiers in the east are more attracted to stiffer racing-style skis because they grab well in the ice, whereas tree fans who love powder and bumps may want something a little softer. Your skis and boots are very personal so shop around, listen to what the shop assistants tell you, and try on several pairs. Demo skis are usually available at resorts.

Snowboard technology is also advancing – the new clip in/out bindings mean less time spent sitting manually adjusting them, though not everyone is happy with this new style. It is perhaps even more important for boarders than for skiers to consider what sort of style they enjoy. Racing boards are certainly different from those designed for pipes and shorter boards are easier to jump around with. Find a pair of boots that is comfortable – of course compared to ski boots, boarding footwear is pure luxury – then rent a few boards in order to find your style.

New skiers and boarders are in the most difficult situation as they are likely to improve at a fast pace. The fairly new parabolic skis seem to make turns easier but are more trouble in trees and over bumps.

If you're thinking about changing to a whole new type of ski or a very different length, it is probably worth spending the extra $50 and renting a pair of performance skis for a day. (Try to get the demos for free). If you're thinking about shaped skis you may even want a lesson on how to ski on them.

The best advice for boots is to find a shop that guarantees their comfort. Ski boots are by their very nature uncomfortable, so when trying them on think of spending a whole day with your foot locked in. Certain makes seem to favour different shaped feet. For example, Salamon fits a generally wider foot, while Langes fit ones narrower. Regardless of your skiing ability, buy your boots to last. They will often cost more than your skis and should serve you well for several years. Any boots up around the $500 mark should have mouldable inserts and it is important to measure the shell without the liner as the plastic will not change shape.

❏ Ice Climbing
With all the cliff faces and mountains that there are in Canada, it is easy to understand why climbing has become such a popular sport, however there is a group of hard core vertical fans who have decided to climb year-round. Ice climbing is growing in popularity and all major resorts and most cities have outfitting shops. This sport even makes skiing seem affordable…and safe!

Poles are also very personal, but not worth spending too much on. If you don't ski forward enough, or have a habit of standing straight up, you may want to try slightly shorter poles.

To get totally outfitted can cost upwards of $1000 for fairly good equipment, so it is worth keeping your skis tuned and not leaving your boots unclipped in the garage as they will lose their shape. Have a good idea of what sort of skiing you enjoy and don't get talked into a pair of $700 racing skis. People often spend far too much on equipment they will never really use. An advanced all-around skier still does not warrant competition-class downhill skis and the best, stiffest racing boots are not necessarily the pair you want on all day.

CLOTHING

The bad news is that ski fashions are always changing and outfits are never cheap. The good news is that on most Canadian hills no one cares what you look like. In fact well-dressed people struggling down the bunny (nursery) slopes are generally a source of amusement and are presumed to be wealthy tourists. If you do enjoy the finer things in life you'll feel more comfortable in a place like Whistler in BC than in a smaller resort. Banff, too, has its share of well-equipped and outfitted visitors, but manages to maintain a relaxed feel.

Clothing should always be warm and those skiing near the coast will appreciate waterproofs. First-time visitors to the Rockies may not have skied in such cold weather before and should certainly be prepared. Essentially covering all exposed skin is the way to go as the air is so dry it won't get through to your skin. The coldest parts of any day are the long trips on the chairs; the new quads make the journey faster but cause more wind chill. To keep as warm as possible skiers often cover their faces for the journey up.

Skiing anywhere near the St Lawrence in Québec can mean being exposed to very cold winds blowing off the river. While covering up is still the best course of action, this is a humid cold so it can find its way through the best jacket. Average temperatures are higher, so the cold is generally not a big problem, but you may want to reconsider skiing on the extremely cold days as the heavy snow remains crusty.

One-piece suits are great, although somewhat job specific. Most skiers opt for a good, longer jacket and a pair of leg warmers. Many jackets now have several sections so you can remove layers when the day warms up. The old stretchy pants have gone out of fashion – they were never warm enough and it was about time people stopped trying to show off a figure in winter apparel. Some skiers get cold feet regardless of how good their boots are. Extra insulating pads can be inserted under the lining for around $60 and one-day toe and hand warmers usually sell for $1.50. Ears should be covered, although ear muffs can give a false sense of warmth. Something for the neck and chin is a good idea. Hands will almost always need covering and mittens are warmer than gloves.

Boarders need to invest in good gloves or mitts with long wrist-guards as their hands touch the snow frequently. Good waterproof pants are also a must as boarders spend much of the day sitting in snow. Loose clothing seems to be the most popular and as the board forces your feet apart there is little worry of being tangled up.

❏ Snowblades

As more and more skiers will have noticed, the new fad is Snowblades – tiny skis with both ends turned up. At first you may ask yourself why? But you need only look to the streets to see people risking their limbs on in-line skates to find the origin of this new sport. Of course after you've finished laughing at the little skis, watch someone fly down the most difficult of runs with the greatest of ease and perhaps they'll become a little more appealing.

EYEWEAR

Of all the equipment you put on, something for your eyes is the most important. Whether you choose goggles or sunglasses, your eyes must be covered all day. Even in the shade, the glare of snow can do damage and can lead to short-term snow blindness. When the sun is out, eyes can burn in minutes and the damage is irreparable. Make sure your eyewear has UV protection (this is now government regulated) and not too much light can enter from the side. Goggles, particularly those with padding, are much warmer than sunglasses.

The same sun that burns your eyes will also burn your skin, so sunscreen/sunblock has also become a must for all skiers. It's vital even on cloudy days.

Fitness and health

FITNESS

Both skiing and boarding are physically demanding sports and there is no doubt that everyone performs better when in good physical condition. People of all ages can enjoy skiing and you don't have to be a perfect physical specimen in order to visit the mountains. Nevertheless, injuries are more likely if you push your body beyond its natural limitations. Knee and shoulder injuries occur frequently and collarbone fractures are also quite common among snowboarders because their arms provide the first line of defence when falling.

Collisions remain by far the largest source of skiing and boarding injuries. While most collisions can be avoided some contact between skiers and the mountain is inevitable. If you're skiing among trees you must remain in control. On busy slopes all skiers and riders must be responsibly aware of others around them. It is dangerous to simply stop in the middle of a run, particularly on the down side of a bump. Boarders sitting down can be very hard to see. Overall, if you are being safe and aware you should never collide with anything or anyone. If you are starting to fall it is sometimes best just to let it happen. When falling, remain relaxed and don't fight the impact – snow isn't too hard!

As skiing is an outdoor winter sport stretching is fundamental to safety and performance. A good stretch after a day out also quickens recovery time. Drinking beer all night in a hot tub is not good preparation for the following day's fun! As a seasonal activity it is unlikely most skiers and riders will use the same muscles in the same sequence year round, so allow for a few slower days at the beginning of the season. The following is a suggested outline of activities which will help to prepare you for the slopes.

PRE-SEASON EXERCISES

Certainly any general fitness program will keep you in good shape but will not prepare you specifically for skiing. Cyclists and joggers will feel their exercise has paid off, but will nevertheless notice unused muscles when they return to their skis. Mountain hiking is excellent, particularly downhill walking.

Skiing and boarding put a lot of stress on your legs and thigh muscles are expected to perform for extended periods in an extended flex position. Wall squats with your legs bent and your back against the wall are a great exercise. Don't ever bounce, but once you can sustain this position for several minutes you can start sliding your back up and down against the wall. Squats with weights are also excellent, but must be done correctly. Lunges (stepping forward and bending your knee while keeping your hips straight) can be done in the gym or on a couple of stairs in your house.

Calves also need attention, particularly for snowboarders. A good all around exercise is to raise up on your toes while keeping your back straight, then bend your knees to a squatting position. Stand back up and then drop back to your heels. This should be done slowly and you can close your eyes to further practise balance.

Trunk strengthening is very important. Your mid-section will absorb everything your legs don't – moguls are particularly tough on the lower back. Always bend your knees when doing sit-ups. Hanging from a bar and lifting your knees slowly is good for your abdomen, shoulders and back.

Obviously any overall weight and fitness program will help you as an athlete. Just remember to work on muscular endurance and remain relaxed and well stretched. Any activity which develops balance will pay off on the slopes.

DURING THE SEASON

Regardless of how often you ski, stretching is vital. At the beginning of the day, remember the air is probably cold and so are your muscles. Stretch your calves, quads, hamstrings and hips for 20-30 seconds each and give your shoulders a good 10-second stretch in several positions. Also stretch out your mid-section and generally loosen up

❑ CODE OF CONDUCT FOR SKIERS AND BOARDERS

The following is a general code of which all or some has been accepted and is applied at all Canadian resorts. Enforcement of this code is the responsibility of individual resorts which retain the right to unilaterally revoke lift tickets and expel and ban offending skiers or boarders from resorts.

Every skier is required to:
1. Obey the signs.
2. Yield the right of way to skiers downhill and choose a course that does not jeopardize their safety.
3. Yield the right of way to skiers uphill when entering a slope and at intersections.
4. Use skis equipped with safety edges and a braking system.
5. When stopping on a slope, the skier must be visible to skiers uphill and ensure that he/she is not obstructing the slope.

It is prohibited for any skier to:
1. Make a fast downhill run.
2. Make jumps.
3. Ski outside the designated ski slopes.
4. Ski on closed slopes.
5. Ski while wearing a Walkman or other audio equipment.
6. Cross the track of a surface ski lift in operation.
7. Remove any signs.
8. Leave the site of an accident in which he/she is involved without identifying himself to a first-aider.

Responsibilities
There are obvious responsibilities an individual accepts when participating in alpine or cross-country skiing. Advanced skiers have a responsibility to the less experienced and in turn novice skiers should master stopping before leaving beginner slopes. If you are a tree fan, or want to experience more remote areas of a mountain, you should always ski with a partner as ski patrols cannot continuously cover a whole mountain.

Skiing beyond boundaries is always prohibited, but the reality is that skiers continue to do so. If you like slightly wilder terrain and insist on exploring unpatrolled areas you should never go alone and should have some sort of avalanche training.

The nature of snowboarding means spending significant amounts of time sitting on the snow, while this is of course fine, large groups of boarders have caused serious accidents by not being visible. Being aware of the whole mountain and the other people on it is every skier's and boarder's responsibility.

your whole body. Your first two or three runs should be fairly easy ones. If you get tired during the day, have a rest. Form is very important when skiing and fatigue leads to laziness and accidents. This is why you stayed in shape all summer!

At the end of the day do some stretching again and enjoy a good hot tub – this is a great place for stretching. If you're skiing the following day, a good night's sleep is important. After a ski weekend allow your body a couple of recovery days before going to the gym.

Although downhill skiing and snowboarding are outdoor sports with inherent risks, rates of injury are fairly low; with a bit of luck, and some thought for safety, it is possible to ski for years on all types of terrain with little more than the odd bruise.

HEALTHCARE

Canada has a system of socialised medicine which is regulated by the Canada Health Act. Health care is a provincial matter and Canadians visiting other provinces for less then 12 months are covered by their own province. Since more provinces have reciprocal payment agreements individuals need simply show their health care card. Québec has not signed this agreement so out of province Canadians may be billed directly and will need to have their money refunded in their own province.

Non-Canadians must have medical insurance. It is up to individual doctors and hospitals whether they bill individuals or their insurance companies. Generally, for short visits individuals will be billed directly. If it is not an emergency it is much less expensive to go to a doctor's office than to a hospital. A trip to Banff Hospital for example will cost over $200, whereas a local clinic will charge less than $30. Medication is always paid for at the pharmacy and receipts are then claimed back from insurance.

❏ **Trail grading**
The standard system of trail grading is used on the maps throughout this book. Note, however, the box item, 'What is a Black Run' (p18).
- ● Beginner trail (green run)
- ■ Intermediate trail (blue run)
- ◆ Advanced trail (black run)
- ◆◆ Expert trail (double black run)

Skiing BC

British Columbia (BC) is Canada's third largest, third most populous and second wealthiest province and the superlatives available to describe this magnificent place are simply too few. BC is the most westerly province covering nearly a million acres and it resembles an accordion held together by the Pacific Ocean on one side and the rest of Canada on the other. As a result of the Pacific plate being thrust under the giant North American plate, 70% of BC consists of high mountains and narrow valleys.

British Columbia's diversity is staggering and much of the north is still only accessible by foot or helicopter. The southern interior, however, is dotted with towns and small cities – many of which have ski fields nearby. Of the province's almost four million inhabitants half live in the lower mainland (the area around Vancouver) and 300,000 can be found on Vancouver Island, mostly in and around Victoria, the very British capital.

It is fair to say that British Columbia offers the greatest diversity of skiing opportunities in Canada, from the thick wet snow of Vancouver Island to the deep powder of the interior. The true skier does not need to look beyond this province, although an excursion into the Alberta side of the Rockies is always tempting. British Columbia has no less than 20 significant, and numerous smaller, alpine ski destinations. As much of the province is a series of valleys, resorts tend to be grouped together naturally, with similar conditions and terrain. The opportunities for cross-country and back-country fans are almost limitless. For the true expert there are several locations that offer Canada's best selection of heli-skiing.

CLIMATE

British Columbia, particularly the inhabited southern areas, has the most varied climate of any province in Canada. Each of the interior valleys has its own weather system with varying levels of precipitation and vastly different average temperatures. On balance though, British Columbians enjoy milder winters than the inhabitants of the other western provinces – Vancouver Island is the mildest place in the country.

GETTING AROUND BC

Due to the diverse and mountainous nature of BC, direct travel in any direction is almost impossible. The province is traversed by the Trans-Canada Highway and the drive from Vancouver to the centre of the Okanagan has been considerably shortened by the construction of Canada's first toll highway, the Coquihalla ($10). This superhighway has been built across the top of the coastal mountains and **can be treacherous during winter storms!**

Roads are well maintained and patrolled but can be closed almost everywhere after huge snowfalls or due to avalanche threats. Snow tunnels have been erected along many of the higher passes and the gravel trucks are busy all winter. Nonetheless it is still recommended and indeed required in some places to have good winter tires and/or chains.

One of the real pleasures of driving around BC is the government supported signposting which makes almost every destination easy to find. This is bound to change over the next few years as service providers are now required to pay for signs themselves. If the roads are clear resist the urge to speed as the police in BC are vigilant and maintain a zero tolerance policy towards speeding. While speed limits vary, 90km/h tends to be the limit on roads that would be 100km/h further east.

Distances in BC are huge. From Vancouver to the Alberta border is at least eight hours and it would take a couple of full days to reach the Yukon. Due to the province's many valleys, north-south travel is generally easy year round and only becomes difficult when crossing passes.

For the skier with money, flying around the province is a good option – particularly as many of the ski centres offer transportation to and from the airport. Obviously the principal port of entry for out of province and international visitors is Vancouver where connecting to regional airports is generally easy. The regional airports at Kelowna and Cranbrook help avoid very long drives.

❏ **TOURISM BRITISH COLUMBIA**
☎ 250-387-1642 or ☎ 1-800-663-6000
Parliament Buildings
Victoria
British Columbia V8V 1X4

Skiing Vancouver

Nestled between the coastal mountains and the Pacific Ocean, Vancouver is undoubtedly one of North America's premier cities and it maintains a wonderful mix between wild Canadian nature and west coast sophistication. The city is developing into one of the most ethnically mixed and culturally varied cities in Canada. From a sporting point of view, this is one of those rare places where one could ski and sail on the same day. There are three ski areas close to the city and Vancouver is the gateway to Whistler/Blackcomb, one of the world's top-rated resorts.

Should you happen to be spending some time in Vancouver in the middle of winter there are a few facts you will likely become aware of: it rains a lot, and sometimes that rain turns to heavy, wet snow; there are far fewer tourists compared with summer; and, most important of all, there is surprisingly good skiing within 30 minutes of the city centre. The problem with skiing around Vancouver is the warmer temperatures and thus a lack of good snow, however the city's three main ski areas are all atop the surrounding mountains and seem to just squeeze into the snow zone.

As a city with a conglomerate population of nearly two million, Vancouver is the west coast's centre for just about everything and the first time visitor may want to invest in a good guidebook and perhaps a separate guide to eating in Vancouver as the diversity of restaurants is in strong competition with Montréal.

The local ski areas are not terribly large but the popularity of the sport means each resort has a reasonable variety of runs and fairly good lifts. The fact that these hills are small is probably due to British Columbia's geography, but they are still worth a mention. Each of the ski areas is located north of Vancouver.

GROUSE MOUNTAIN
Known as the Peak of Vancouver, Grouse is also the area that can be seen most easily from the city; if you take the gondola up on a clear day the views alone are almost worth the cost of the ticket. The constant expansion atop Grouse has transformed the

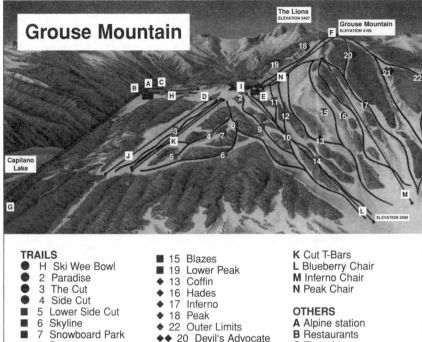

TRAILS

● H Ski Wee Bowl
● 2 Paradise
● 3 The Cut
● 4 Side Cut
■ 5 Lower Side Cut
■ 6 Skyline
■ 7 Snowboard Park
■ 8 Buckhorn
■ 9 Centennial
■ 10 Expo
■ 11 Deliverance
■ 12 Tyee Chute
■ 14 Blue Face

■ 15 Blazes
■ 19 Lower Peak
◆ 13 Coffin
◆ 16 Hades
◆ 17 Inferno
◆ 18 Peak
◆ 22 Outer Limits
◆◆ 20 Devil's Advocate
◆◆ 21 Purgatory

LIFTS

H Ski Wee Bowl
I Paradise Rope Tow
J Cut Chair

K Cut T-Bars
L Blueberry Chair
M Inferno Chair
N Peak Chair

OTHERS

A Alpine station
B Restaurants
C First aid
D Ski school/rentals/repairs
E Peak office
F Peak patio
G Valley station

❑ GROUSE MOUNTAIN
Base elevation: 781m (2,500ft)
Summit: 1,281m (4,100ft)
Vertical: 500m (1,600ft)
Lifts: 1 gondola, 4 doubles and 6 surface
22 runs: 30% beginner, 50% intermediate, 20% advanced
Average snowfall: 250cm (98in)
Lift operating hours: weekdays 9am-10pm, weekends 8am-10pm

Contacts
Information and reservations: ☎ 604-984-0661
Snow phone: ☎ 604-986-6262
Guest services (Ski school and Pass information): ☎ 604-980-9311
Home page: www.grousemtn.com

area from a small ski hill into a year-round tourist destination. As a result a variety of activities are now available and the wood carvings (at the base of the gondola and up at the Lodge) are worth a look. The most difficult aspect of skiing Grouse is the unpredictable snow and a season that can begin as late as the new year.

Grouse has enough varied skiing to fill a day and its proximity to the city can't be beaten. The mountain has the full spread of options for lessons as well as affordable rentals. There are also a few kilometres of cross-country tracks. With its night skiing (13 lifts are open) and good dinners, Grouse becomes an appealing after work option, particularly since it is just 10 minutes from downtown – providing the traffic over Lion's Gate Bridge is flowing smoothly. Even if Vancouver is foggy it's likely to be clear at Grouse, however since the conditions at the top are not always clear from the gondola base you should ask before you go up. Due to the warm weather the snow can be slushy.

Cypress Bowl – Mt Strachan

TRAILS
- 12 Collins
- 20 Runway
- 23 Shuttle
- 3 T-33
- 5 Horizon
- 10 Cat-Track
- 11 Hutch
- 24 Half Pipe
- 25 Lower Bowen
- 1 Top Gun
- 2 Rip-Cord
- 4 Humpty Dumpty
- 6 Gibsons
- 7 Rainbow
- 8 Bowen
- 9 Slash
- 22 Tomcat

LIFTS
A Sky Chair
B Sunrise quad Chair
C Easy-Rider Tow
D Midway Chair

OTHERS
F Ticket office/Ski school
G Ski rental
H Café/Lounge
I Parking
J Ski patrol
K Permanent closure
L Area boundary

CYPRESS BOWL

The smallest of Vancouver's resorts in area, Cypress Bowl has a good lift system and great snow accumulations. Along with the entertaining alpine runs, it also has some of the best cross country in the area with 23 tracks, six of which (all green runs) are lit at night. To reach Cypress Bowl drive south from West Vancouver along the Trans-Canada and follow the signs to Cypress Bowl Provincial Park. From Vancouver drive north on Highway 99.

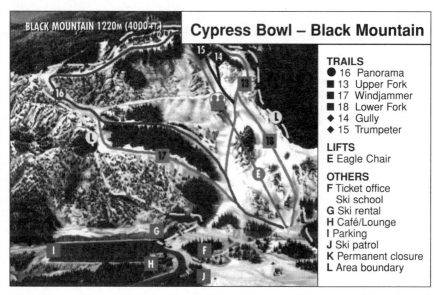

Cypress Bowl – Black Mountain

BLACK MOUNTAIN 1220m (4000 ft)

TRAILS
● 16 Panorama
■ 13 Upper Fork
■ 17 Windjammer
■ 18 Lower Fork
◆ 14 Gully
◆ 15 Trumpeter

LIFTS
E Eagle Chair

OTHERS
F Ticket office
  Ski school
G Ski rental
H Café/Lounge
I Parking
J Ski patrol
K Permanent closure
L Area boundary

The skiing at Cypress is typical bowl skiing with some glades and a fair variety of runs. Runs descend down two sides of the bowl with the cross-country area rounding it out. Cypress is popular with boarders due to the generous snowfalls. As with the other mountainous areas north of Vancouver, the views are superb on a clear day.

Lift tickets (full day)

Adult	Youth (13-18)	Child (6-12)	Senior (65+)	Infant (0-5)
$33	$20	$17	$15	$2

❏ **CYPRESS BOWL**
Base elevation: 980m (3,136ft)
Summit: 1,450m (4,750ft)
Vertical: 470m (1,504ft)
Lifts: 1 quad, 3 doubles, 1 surface
23 runs: 4 beginner, 9 intermediate, 10 advanced
Average snowfall: 500cm (196in)

Contacts
Information and reservations: ☎ 604-926-5612
Snow phone: ☎ 604-419-7669
Cross country information, rentals and ski school: ☎ 604-922-0825
Ski school: ☎ 604-926-5346
Shuttle bus service: ☎ 604-878-9229
Home page: www.cypressbowl.com

Cypress Bowl – Hollyburn

HOLLYBURN PEAK 1326m (4350 ft.)

TRAILS (CROSS COUNTRY)

- 6 Five Lakes
- 13 Sitzmark
- 17 Wells Gray – Lower
- 18 Hollyburn
- 19 Burfield
- 20 Powerline – Lower
- 21 Telemark – Lower
- 23 Short cut
- 3 Triangle Lake
- 4 Unknown Lake
- 5 Powerline – Upper
- 10 Telemark – Upper
- 11 Wells Gray – Upper
- 12 Brothers Canyon West
- 14 West Lake
- 15 Jack Pratt
- 16 Pacific
- 22 Grand National
- ◆ 1 Upper Romstad
- ◆ 2 Romstad
- ◆ 7 Russel
- ◆ 8 Mobraaten
- ◆ 9 Pop Fly

OTHERS

A Ski shop
B Lodge
C Upper warming hut
D Snowplay and toboggan area
E Area boundary
24 Hikers Access

MOUNT SEYMOUR

With the most diversified skiing close to Vancouver, Mount Seymour is ½ hour from downtown heading west along highway #1. Like Cypress Bowl, the ski area is at the top of the road nestled partially in a bowl. The area is part of a provincial park with good summer hiking and winter snowshoeing. Skiing has being enjoyed on Mount Seymour since the 1930s; the first lift was constructed in 1949.

Seymour is a popular spot with snowboarders as it has three purpose-built parks. The older style glades which run off the Mystery Peak chair are good fun. Mount Seymour has three lifts which are good for newer skiers and the two higher chairs allow for more varied terrain. The mountain also has an area for tubing and has a few runs with night skiing.

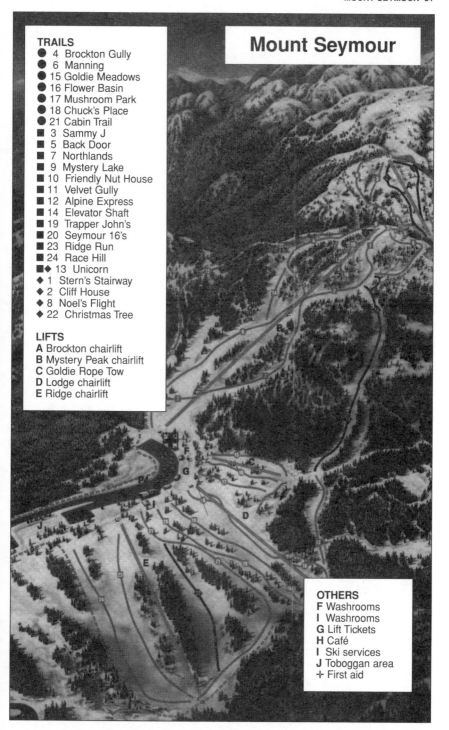

Mount Seymour

TRANS
● 4 Brockton Gully
● 6 Manning
● 15 Goldie Meadows
● 16 Flower Basin
● 17 Mushroom Park
● 18 Chuck's Place
● 21 Cabin Trail
■ 3 Sammy J
■ 5 Back Door
■ 7 Northlands
■ 9 Mystery Lake
■ 10 Friendly Nut House
■ 11 Velvet Gully
■ 12 Alpine Express
■ 14 Elevator Shaft
■ 19 Trapper John's
■ 20 Seymour 16's
■ 23 Ridge Run
■ 24 Race Hill
■◆ 13 Unicorn
◆ 1 Stern's Stairway
◆ 2 Cliff House
◆ 8 Noel's Flight
◆ 22 Christmas Tree

LIFTS
A Brockton chairlift
B Mystery Peak chairlift
C Goldie Rope Tow
D Lodge chairlift
E Ridge chairlift

OTHERS
F Washrooms
I Washrooms
G Lift Tickets
H Café
I Ski services
J Toboggan area
✛ First aid

❏ MOUNT SEYMOUR
Base elevation: 1,010m (3,240ft)
Summit: 1,400m (4,500ft)
Vertical: 390m (1,250ft)
Lifts: 4 chairs, 2 surface
20 runs: 40% beginner, 40% intermediate, 20% advanced
Average snowfall: 400cm (157in)

Contacts
Information and reservations: ☎ 604-986-2261 (Vancouver) or ☎ 604-872-6616 (from Fraser valley)
Snow phone: ☎ 604-879-3999
Home page: www.mountseymour.com

HEMLOCK VALLEY RESORT

As you drive east from Vancouver the mountains rise up in the distance like a wall separating the green, wet lower mainland from the rest of the country. These mountains are part of a chain which descend south to the ski areas of Washington State. The first resort that skiers will encounter is the little known Hemlock Valley Resort. Nestled in a bowl on the north side of the Fraser Valley, Hemlock has been a popular centre for years with local skiers and The Sasquatch. Otherwise known as Big Foot this legendary creature (a sort of gorilla-man) is said to roam the surrounding hills.

Most of Hemlock's skiing is above the trees with some good, longer intermediate terrain off the Sasquatch triple. Beginners get the smaller lifts or have the option of riding up the Skyline double with the advanced skiers and taking the one easier route down. This is a great place to learn to ski powder when there is a heavy accumulation.

Snowboarding

Although Hemlock has a good snowboard park and half-pipe off the Sasquatch chair, the open bowl has made the whole area popular with boarders.

Cross country

There are seven kilometres of track-set, cross-country trails at the base of the slopes with a training centre and a biathlon shooting range. Rentals and lessons are available Equipment rental for adults (13+) for one day costs $12 (half day $9); 12 and under $8 (half day $6). A private lesson (one hour) is $32 for one person and $18 for a second person). A day pass costs $8 and a season pass $59 (seniors over 65 and children

❏ HEMLOCK VALLEY
Base elevation: 975m (3,130ft)
Summit: 1,323m (4,230ft)
Vertical: 348m (1,150ft)
Lifts: 1 triple, 2 doubles, 1 surface (two more lifts are planned)
34 runs: 8 beginner, 11 intermediate, 15 advanced
Average snowfall: 4m (13ft)
Lift operating hours: 9am-3.30pm (8pm on Fridays)

Contacts
Information and reservations: ☎ 604-797-4411
24hr snow phone: ☎ 1-800-665-7080

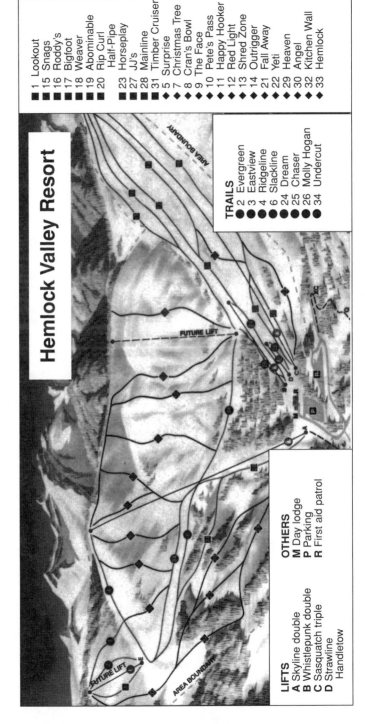

Hemlock Valley Resort

■ 1 Lookout
■ 15 Snags
■ 16 Roddy's
■ 17 Bigfoot
■ 18 Weaver
■ 19 Abominable
■ 20 Rip Curl
   Half-Pipe
■ 23 Horseplay
■ 27 JJ's
■ 28 Mainline
■ 31 Timber Cruiser
◆ 5 Surprise
◆ 7 Christmas Tree
◆ 8 Cran's Bowl
◆ 9 The Face
◆ 10 Pete's Pass
◆ 11 Happy Hooker
◆ 12 Red Light
◆ 13 Shred Zone
◆ 14 Outrigger
◆ 21 Fall Away
◆ 22 Yeti
◆ 29 Heaven
◆ 30 Angel
◆ 32 Kitchen Wall
◆ 33 Hemlock

TRAILS
● 2 Evergreen
● 3 Eastview
● 4 Ridgeline
● 6 Slackline
● 24 Dream
● 25 Chaser
● 26 Molly Hogan
● 34 Undercut

LIFTS
A Skyline double
B Whistlepunk double
C Sasquatch triple
D Strawline
   Handletow

OTHERS
M Day lodge
P Parking
R First aid patrol

aged 5 and under ski free). A Never Ever package including trail ticket, rental and a 1¹/₂hr private lesson is $29. The trails are open from 9am-3.30pm.

Lessons and rentals

Group lessons (1¹/₂ hours, 10 people) are $18 for skiers and boarders (a package of four lessons costs $59). Private lessons (one hour) cost $32 ($18 for a second person).

Never Ever inclusive packages (equipment, 1¹/₂ hour lesson, Yellow lift ticket) are $29 for skiers and $44 for snowboarders. The same package but with an All area lift ticket costs $49 for skiers and $59 for snowboarders.

Equipment can be rented by the day, half day or night. Downhill skis for anyone over 13 cost $19 per day, for children (6-12) $12, and for those aged 5 and under, $10. Reservations are required for snowboard hire; a board and boot cost $30 per day.

Lift tickets

	Adult	Youth (13-17)	Child (6-12)
Full day	$30	$25	$16
Half day	$24	$20	$14
Night skiing	$10	$10	$10

Half-day tickets are valid between 12 noon and 3.30pm. Seniors (65+) ski free here and there is night skiing on Fridays (3.30-8pm).

Getting there and around

Hemlock is 40km east of Agassiz on the north side of the Fraser, off highway #7. The resort is about 125km east of Vancouver and can be driven to in under two hours. The area is the most convenient resort for the cities of the lower mainland such as Chilliwack, Abbotsford and Hope.

Accommodation and après ski

Hemlock has a few privately-owned condos at the base of the hill, some of which can be rented. For reservations phone (☎ 604-797-4411).

Accommodation and a wide selection of restaurants are available throughout the area; nearby **Harrison Hot Springs** is a good spot for some R&R. A visit to nearby **Hope** is also worthwhile for a look at the many wood carvings the town has become famous for.

MANNING PARK

Over 200km east of Vancouver along the southern Hope-Princeton highway, Manning Park Resort is in a quiet provincial park with fantastic snow and good skiing. This is a small, well-maintained area with few of the trappings of the more major resorts. Consequently there is a relaxed feel and prices are affordable. Since the construction

---

❑ MANNING PARK
Base elevation: 1,353m (4,451ft)
Summit: 1,790m (5,868ft)
Vertical: 437m (1,417ft)
Lifts: 2 doubles, 2 surface
24 runs: 30% novice, 40% intermediate, 30% advanced
Average snowfall: 535cm (214in)

Contacts
Information and reservations: ☎ 250-840-8822
Snow phone: ☎ 604-878-8900

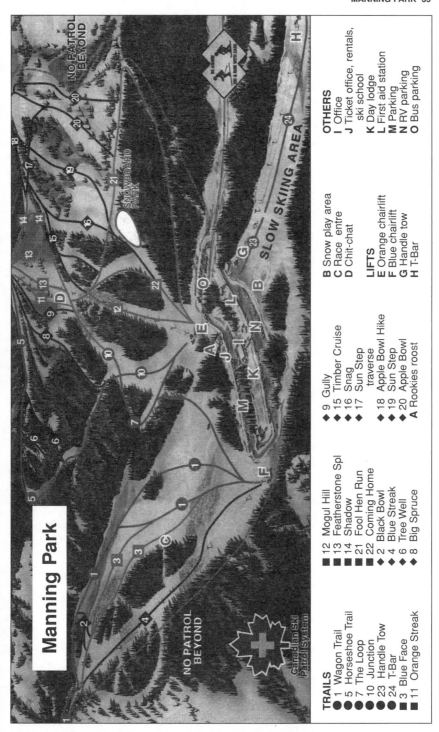

Manning Park

NO PATROL BEYOND

NO PATROL BEYOND

NO PATROL BEYOND

Canadian Ski Patrol System

SLOW SKIING AREA

SNOWBOARD PARK

TRAILS
● 1 Wagon Trail
● 5 Horseshoe Trail
● 7 The Loop
● 10 Junction
● 23 Handle Tow
● 24 T-Bar
■ 3 Blue Face
■ 11 Orange Streak
■ 12 Mogul Hill
■ 13 Featherstone Spl
■ 14 Shadow
■ 21 Fool Hen Run
■ 22 Coming Home
◆ 2 Black Bowl
◆ 4 Blue Streak
◆ 6 Tree Well
◆ 8 Big Spruce
◆ 9 Gully
◆ 15 Timber Cruise
◆ 16 Snag
◆ 17 Sun Step traverse
◆ 18 Apple Bowl Hike
◆ 19 Sun Step
◆ 20 Apple Bowl
A Rookies roost

B Snow play area
C Race entre
D Chit-chat

LIFTS
E Orange chairlift
F Blue chairlift
G Handle tow
H T-Bar

OTHERS
I Office
J Ticket office, rentals, ski school
K Day lodge
L First aid station
M Parking
N RV parking
O Bus parking

of the Coquihalla super highway, Manning Park has become even quieter, so it makes for an even more relaxing break.

Manning Park has a totally independent beginner area so there is little chance of being buzzed by faster skiers. The Blue chair has a slightly bumpy advanced run, but is generally a good area for beginners and budding intermediates. The Orange chair has good advanced runs through the trees. Snowfalls are good and the mountain remains fairly uncrowded.

Snowboarding
There is a snowboard park off the Fool Hen Run. The snow is good for boards and the trees hold it well.

Cross country
There are seven kilometres of track-set trails in the park with all levels of difficulty. The Nordic Centre is down closer to the highway and there are many other back-country options in the area. Trail passes cost $11.50 for adults, $10.50 for youth (13-17), $8.50 for juniors (7-12), $9.50 for seniors (65+) – children aged 6 and under ski free.

Lessons and rentals
Inclusive packages – equipment, lesson (1½ hour) and pass – start as low as $40 ($50 for more advanced skiers). Snowboard lessons cost $55. Manning Park also offers a variety of Kinderski programs for kids of all ages and levels, as well as cross-country courses. Telemarking is also popular and lessons are available.

Ski and boot rentals start at around $21 per day. Boards with boots can be hired for $36.

Lift tickets
Full day, mid-week tickets cost $19 per person. On weekends and holidays the price goes up to $30 for adults and $24 for youths.

Getting there and around
The resort is 45 minutes east of Hope along Highway #3. Conditions can be a little icy in winter, though they are even worse further east. It takes close to three hours to drive from Vancouver.

Accommodation
The village area is a few kilometres from the slopes and the majority of accommodation is simple and unpretentious. For reservations phone ☎ 250-840-8822.

The Main Lodge has rooms from $65 per couple and cabins large enough for 10 people are as low as $250 a night. The Ski Lodge has a BBQ and a café. The Lodge has a good dining room, a lounge and a small store.

Whistler/Blackcomb

Just 114km of beautiful driving north of Vancouver brings you to Whistler, Canada's premier ski resort and one of the world's most highly rated ski destinations. However, as you walk through the chic pedestrianized streets it's hard to imagine you're in Canada. Although the area has had some tourism since early this century, Whistler's roots date back to 1966 and in real terms the two mountain resort dates only from the early 1980s.

For Canadians who grew up skiing on undiscovered mountains with one rustic little lodge, the Whistler statistics are incredible and perhaps a touch ominous. Since 1975 over $2.6 billion has been poured into the resort and the investment seems to have paid off. There are over 37,000 bed units and almost 16,000 more to come – the highest amount of ski-in/ski-out accommodation in North America! During the 1996/97 season the two mountains hosted 1.74 million skiers. That's nearly half the population of BC!

One of the pleasures of skiing Whistler/Blackcomb is the variety of places from which one can approach the slopes. While there is the central village, there are also two other development areas, each with access to the mountains. For those who enjoy exploring, it is possible to travel from one extreme end of the resort to the other and back again without walking more than a few metres!

A cynic may feel as though Whistler is simply one big condo development, however the resort demonstrates a great deal of foresight. Literally everything is geared towards the holiday maker. In fact 90% of the people walking around are tourists and an enormous proportion of those employed on the hills or in the shops are young members of the Commonwealth on working holiday visas. The few people who actually own the fantastic homes do not tend to have major financial concerns – even a basic two-bedroom condo is more expensive than an average house in Toronto or Vancouver.

As an international destination the two mountains are first class and have by far the best lift system in Canada. The combined lift capacity is over 42,000 skiers and boarders an hour! Unfortunately no mountain can possibly be big enough to hide that many people. Even though the resort does constitute two distinct mountains, your lift ticket is good on both and it is possible to ski both mountains on the same day. However, keep in mind that from the top of Blackcomb to the top of Whistler can take a good hour. As a result of high verticals and a wonderful diversity of terrain coupled with the excellent lift system, good skiing is available throughout Whistler's extended season. However, the snow at the bottom can become a little slushy.

To really get to know the whole resort allow at least one week. There seems to be no consistency in who prefers which mountain and locals seem evenly divided. Each has such a variety of terrain that it's often simply more pleasant to ski on the one that is not hosting some competition, or playing loud music around the half-pipe.

❏ **Olympic highs**
Canada's first gold of the 1998 Winter Olympics and the first gold medal ever awarded in snowboarding almost went up in smoke when Whistler's own Ross Rebagliati tested positive – not to anabolic steroids but to a small amount of marijuana. Fortunately for Ross, BC's largest illegal crop is in a bit of a grey area in terms of Olympic rules and most experts agree it does anything but enhance performance.

Whistler

THE WEST IS YET TO COME.
The trails from West Bowl

STEFAN'S CHUTE
STEFAN'S SALUTE
WEST BOWL
Cockalorum
PEAK TO CREEK
SNEAKY PETE
CLIFF AREA
MOTION
DOOM & GLOOM
GRANDE FINALE
PERMANENTLY CLOSED AREA
HIGH SHOULDER
Whistler Mountain Peak Lookout Elevation 7,160 Ft/2,182 M
MID-UNLOAD
WHISTLER BOWL
CLIFF AREA
THE COULOIR
PERMANENTLY CLOSED AREA
THE CIRCUS
PEAK CHAIR
SHALE SLOPE
LEFT HOOK
SURPRISE
FRANZ'S MEADOWS
FRANZ'S
RID O
LAST CHANCE
GLACIER BOWL
THE SADDLE
Little Whistler Peak Elevation 6,930 Ft/2,115 M
T-BARS
T-Bar Run
GUEST SATISFACTION CENTRE
Ski & Snowboard School / Mountain Adventure Centre
PIKA'S & THE ROUNDHOUSE ELEVATION 6,069 Ft/1,850 M
SNOWMAKING RESERVOIR
OLD MAN
BLUERS RESERVOIR
FISHEYE
PORCUPINE
PONY TRAIL
BIG RED EXPRESS
SNOWMOBILE
PAPOOSE
Little Whistler
PIKA'S TRAVERSE
CAMEL HUMPS
RIDGE RUN
BACK BOWL
HALF PIPE
BURNT STEW TRAIL
SYMPHONY BOWL
To Sun Bowl
HARMONY HORSESHOES
MORAINE
HARMONY BOWL
HARMONY PISTE
HARMONY EXPRESS
JOLLY GREEN GIANT
EMERALD EXPRESS
UPPER WHISKEY JACK
ELEVATION 5,528 Ft/1,685 Ft
CRESCENDO
KALEIDESCOPE
KIRKINCOLM
BOOMER BOWL
LOW ROLL
McCONKEY'S
SHOWCASE
SHOWCASE T
GIANT STEPS
RATFINK
GREEN GIANT
RATFINK
SHOWCASE
GARBANZO
CLIFF AREA
TERRAIN PARK
DARK SIDE
DOUBLE TROUBLE
OLMAROT

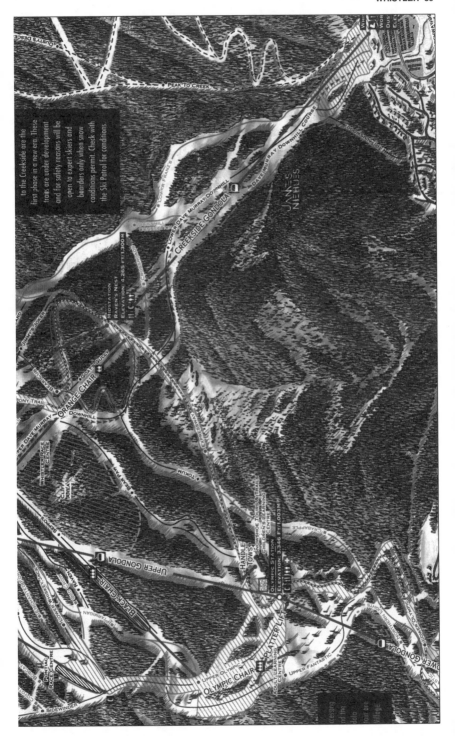

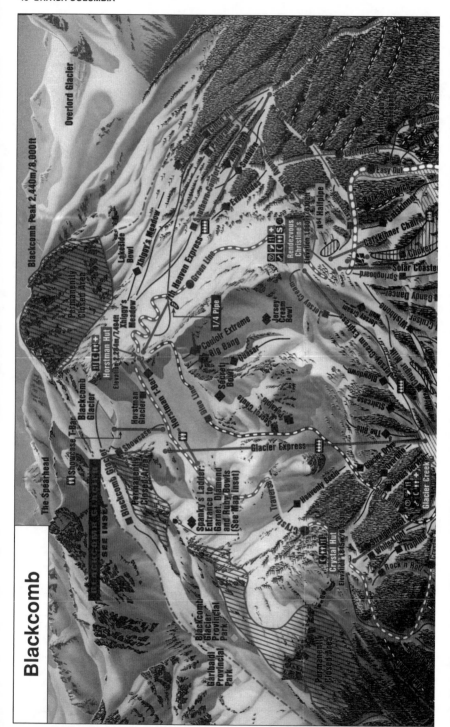

Blackcomb

BLACKCOMB GLACIER

Blackcomb's incredible high-alpine area offers acres of terrain in its natural state. Be aware that rapidly changing weather conditions will increase the difficulty of the terrain. Always ski/ride in control and enter each open gates area only. The Ski Patrol is available to answer any questions you may have.

Horstman Hut
Elevation 2,284m/7,494ft

Children's Adventure Park

Terrain Park

Gear Jammer

Undercut

Lower Gear Jammer

Freefall

Mainline

Wizard Express

Merlins

Springboard

Black Magic

Sorcerer

Grub Stake

Stoker

Green Line

Excalibur Gondola

Cruiser

Express

Stoker Bumps

Cruiser Bumps

Excelerator

Honeycomb

Zig Zag

Buzz Cut

Crystal Chair

Trapline

Kokanee Ski Machine

Beginner Area

Excalibur Base II Station

Blackcomb Glacier Entrance

Horstman Glacier

Horstman T-Bar

Showcase T-Bar

Glacier Express

Spanky's Ladder Entrance to Garnet, Ruby and Diamond Bowls

Garnet Bowl

Ruby Bowl

Blow Hole

Permanently Closed Area

Blackcomb Glacier

Diamond Bowl

Permanently Closed Area

Permanently Closed Area

Blackcomb Glacier Provincial Park

Garibaldi Provincial Park

BLACKCOMB MOUNTAIN

Built in 1980, Blackcomb is the newer of the two resorts that constitute the ski area but is far from being the minor partner. Blackcomb's summit is slightly higher than Whistler's and skiing continues into August, at the very top anyway. The mountain is accessed from two areas; the Blackcomb Daylodge via the two-way covered Wizard Express quad, or from Whistler Village by way of the Excalibur gondola. One of the real pleasures of skiing on a mountain as high and as well thought-out as Blackcomb is the ability to ride to the very top and then descend over two kilometres of challenging and diverse runs. There are a few extremely long and varied green runs which make the entire mountain accessible to almost all abilities, so if you're beyond the rope-tow stage make use of your $55 ticket.

For strong intermediate skiers Seventh Heaven is the big winner, if you can put up with the often high winds at the top of the chair. The sun shines most frequently here and there's always a beautiful view of Whistler. Several runs have been cut for those who love trees but, as is often the case, advanced skiers who enjoy these runs don't always like the extended ski-outs back to the nearest lift.

Blackcomb's advanced terrain is renowned and it is one of the annual hosts of the Extreme Skiing Championships – you know you've skied well if no bones are broken. For those double-black experts who are not competing, your days will be spent above the tree line jumping into high glacial bowls. There are certainly worse ways to spend a day!

WHISTLER MOUNTAIN

There must be a few older souls in Whistler who feel nostalgic about the good old days, however the fortunes they have made from real-estate have surely cured any depression! As with Blackcomb there are two village areas from which to climb the mountain (some literally do this to avoid certain ticket costs!). The gondola from

---

❏ BLACKCOMB MOUNTAIN
Base elevation: 675m (2,214ft)
Summit: 2,284m (7,494ft)
Vertical: 1,609m (5,280ft)
Lifts: 1 gondola, 6 quads (one covered), 3 triples, 7 surface
100+ runs: 15% beginner, 55% intermediate, 30% expert
Average snowfall: 9.14m (30ft) on summit
Lift operating hours: Opening to end January 8.30am-3pm (weekends/holidays) and 9am-3pm midweek; February to end of the season 8.30am-3.30pm (weekends/holidays) and 9am-3.30pm midweek.

❏ WHISTLER MOUNTAIN
Base elevation: 652m (2,140ft)
Summit: 2,182m (7,160ft)
Vertical: 1,530m (5,020ft)
Lifts: 2 gondolas, 3 quads, 3 triples, 1 doubles, 4 surface
100+ runs: 20% beginner, 55% intermediate, 25% expert
Average snowfall: 9.14m (30ft) on summit
Lift operating hours: as for Blackcomb

Contacts
Information and reservations: ☎ 1-800-766-0449, ☎ 604-932-3434 or toll free from Vancouver ☎ 604-664-5614
Accommodation: ☎ 1-800-944-7853 or ☎ 603-938-5758
Snow phone: ☎ 604-932-4211 (Whistler) or ☎ 604-687-75079 (Vancouver)
Ski school (Whistler): ☎ 1-800-766-0448
Home page: www.whistler-blackcomb.com

Whistler village is extremely long and it takes you to all sorts of great skiing; the Olympic station is halfway up.

The other village area is **Creekside**; the fun part about skiing here is that it has the only advanced ski-out on either mountain – there is also an intermediate alternative. But the best bit is the development of some runs which offer a fantastic all-black route from top to bottom.

The Peak triple is the route to the highest point and while there is a mid-unloading station the area at the top is the expert's playground. Beware of that omnipresent wind, you may be blown down while transfixed by the truly magnificent views! Those who do not feel so expert but who love stunning views may want to hang out around the Harmony quad; this reaches a similar elevation and has runs for different abilities, though the area is still not really geared to the beginner. One word of warning – don't go under the rope that says 'cliff', it is very tiring climbing back up!

The chairs covering the middle of the mountain offer runs of all types and keep you out of the wind. This mid-section is also just high enough to avoid the natural early and late season slush which develops around the base. Unfortunately when poor conditions prevail higher up, or on busy days, this area becomes crowded.

Snowboarding

On an average day here one encounters nearly as many boarders as skiers; the sport is clearly preferred by the young and the very international staff of the resort. It is not surprising that Whistler/Blackcomb host just about as many riding events as skiing ones.

It would seem that snowboarding comes somewhat easier to those who haven't grown up on snow and Whistler is a common first ski stop for those visiting Canada.

There are good half-pipes up both mountains and a half-pipe off Seventh Heaven on Blackcomb. Competitions are held often and if you're a traditionalist of either sport you may be put off by the blaring music. Due to the fairly heavy snowfalls the upper bowls can almost seem made for a board and it appears a lot more fun to use the lifts you've paid for rather than spending all day on the edge of a crowded pipe…but perhaps not? Because of the excellent lift system and good run-planning, boarders find themselves walking less than on other hills and it's hard to believe few qualities could be more appealing to those who ride. Lower sections of the mountains can be a bit crusty and a little too groomed for real boarding pleasure but they have proven a good training ground for slalom and downhill racers.

Cross country

A one-day trail pass for the 25km of well-groomed runs costs $10 for adults and $5 for kids. Needless to say everything has been thought of including some lights for the evening; the lights are on every night during the season (December to March). The main trails run around Lost Lake, just down Lost Lake Rd from the Upper Village, and are hemmed in by Château Whistler's golf club. All trails are marked and rated for difficulty. There are a couple of washrooms and a warming hut.

The entire Whistler area is full of good hiking trails which become good cross-country paths during winter. There are several nice trails around Alta Lake and further up the west side of the valley. Back-country fans will also find lots to do, particularly behind the two main mountains. You can ski from a helicopter or hike in – avalanche warnings are posted daily.

Lessons and rentals

With a community of businesses based around skiing, rentals are not hard to find and there seems to be very little variance in the prices, though the base lodges are slightly more expensive. Generally, however, you shouldn't have to pay more than $25 a day for the basic goods, but as your performance increases the price for better equipment rises, topping out at around $45 for skis, boots and poles. Boarding equipment is comparable in price and this is a good resort to try out different styles of boards before buying. Renting for several consecutive days will help to save around $5 per day.

As this resort is geared to everyone's needs there is a myriad of ways to improve one's skiing ability and prices are relatively competitive. Half-day group lessons on both mountains cost $45 whereas the private version is $220. These are but the tip of the iceberg as the many multi-day packages are good value. A four-day lift ticket and lesson package costs $212 for adults. A three full-day beginner program costs $170. Whistler has packages for advanced skiers too. For further details contact the ski school (☎ 1-800-766-0448).

Lift tickets

	Adult	Youth (13-18)/Senior (65+)	Child (7-12)
Full Day	$55	$47	$27
Five-day	$265	$225	$125

Children aged 6 and under ski free. It is also possible to get a half-day ticket. Note that these prices do not include the 7% GST.

Skiing begins at 9am midweek and 8.30am at weekends/holidays, however for $16 extra there is an early morning (7am) fresh-tracks ticket which includes breakfast. When the snow is only average, usually early and late in the season, tickets are reduced a few dollars – however hotels offer big discounts at this time.

Getting there and around

Whistler is roughly two hours north of Vancouver along the beautiful Sea to Sky Highway and although the temptation is to speed your way up to the slopes the road is heavily patrolled and narrow in certain points.

As Whistler is very much a part of the international resort community many people choose to fly here. Vancouver International is the closest airport. Some of the jet-set like to arrive by limousine – your hotel will be happy to book transportation for you; alternatively contact Airport Limousine (☎ 604-273-1331 or ☎ 1-800-278-8742).

Should you choose not to join the stream of beautiful vehicles making the journey there are several options. **Maverick Coach Lines** (Vancouver ☎ 604-255-1171, Whistler ☎ 604-932-5031) is the most affordable option at $32 return. **Premier Transportation Ltd** (Vancouver ☎ 604-266-5386, Whistler ☎ 604-905-0041) does the journey for $45 one way and will pick up and drop off at Vancouver hotels. Perhaps the most enjoyable way to visit Whistler is aboard the once daily **BC Rail** service (☎ 604-984-5246 or ☎ 1-800-663-8238). The service departs North Vancouver at 7am and leaves Whistler at 6.10pm ($29 one way) – the journey takes about two hours.

Orientation On a cloudy day a first time visitor to Whistler may be a little confused by the resort's layout, particularly if they've previously skied in smaller Canadian resorts. However, once the sky clears the two towering ski hills keep everyone well oriented. Aside from a few residential areas, most of Whistler has been well thought out. Somehow the over 7,000 full-time residents have managed to hide themselves in beautiful houses and chalets, or tiny over-priced apartments. Whistler Village is the centre of the resort with the majority of hotels and shops. From there it is a short walk to the Upper Village via the major free parking area – just follow the signs. There is also a market area with fast food and shopping where you may park free for up to two hours. The Upper Village is the site of the new Château Whistler and the Blackcomb Daylodge. The other significant area is Whistler Creekside; the amount of accommodation here is increasing but it still has a slightly more homey feel. Off Highway 99 and winding behind Alta Lake is Alta Lake Rd which leads to several hiking trails, cabins and the youth hostel.

If you choose to stay anywhere central it's easy to get around on foot, but for venturing further afield Whistler has its own local bus system (☎ 604-932-4020). Rides cost $1.50.

Accommodation

Alas, there is a good and a bad side. Starting with the negative, Whistler is easily one of the most expensive places to stay in Canada, though upscale fans of European skiing may find it reasonably affordable. On the up side, Whistler has an awesome and ever-growing amount of night-time shelter and the vast majority of options can be booked easily – for an information pack or to make a reservation phone ☎ 1-800-944-7853 or ☎ 604-938-5758. Hotels may also be contacted directly. Although new places are being built all the time it is important to book well in advance of holiday periods and long weekends.

Some people are very particular about their choice of accommodation, but Whistler's overwhelming sense of direction and newness means that most hotels are quite similar and almost all are clean and well maintained. You really need to decide on your price range and the amenities you require. The hotel to fit your needs is probably somewhere in the resort. The other great attraction is the amount of slopeside accommodation.

Most hotels and condos, apart from those in the budget category, start comfortably above the $100 mark for double occupancy and top out at nearly $700 at the *CP Château Whistler Resort* (☎ 604-938-8000 or ☎ 1-800-606-8244), though reduced rates are available. Prices in the resort average between $200 and $300 per night. However, significant low season discounts exist; try before late December or early spring. Keep in mind that through the summer the resort is just as busy.

In the Whistler Village area you may want to try the very central *Delta Resort* (☎ 604-932-1982) for around $300, or the *Whistler Fairways Hotel* (☎ 604-932-2522) with doubles from $100. Four people can pile into *Aspens* (☎ 604-932-7222) for $450; doubles at *Club Intrawest* (☎ 604-689-8816) are $200 per night. *Whistler Resort and Club* (☎ 604-932-2343) in Creekside starts from $99.

Budget accommodation On the budget side the choices are more limited and you will need to book directly. A dorm bed for around $20 a night can be booked direct at *Hostelling International (Whistler)* (☎ 604-932-5492) or from other hostels worldwide. *UBC Lodge* (☎ 604-932-6604) charges a similar rate, and *Fireside Lodge* (☎ 604-932-4545) has dorm beds for $25-$30. It is imperative to phone these places before arriving as they are often full.

If there are no rooms to be had, or the price is not right, Whistler is close enough to Vancouver to ski for the day!

Après ski

Eating well is easy and fortunately there is enough choice in Whistler to ensure that going out does not need to break the bank. The ever-expanding village has everything from crêpes to five-star restaurants. There are several pubs and bars which are lively well into the night, though the streets tend to quieten down after 11pm. There is no need to eat at the same establishment more than once and because most areas are pedestrian only and close together exploring is easy.

Whistler Village and Village North have the perennial favourites, *McDonald's*, *A&W* and *Domino's Pizza,* along with the essential coffee shops to remind you that you're in BC. For good French cuisine try *Val D'Isère* or the more expensive Italian *Trattoria di Umberto*. The main village area also has a *Hard Rock Café*, and the consistently good *Keg* is an excellent place for a steak. Fans of Japanese food will find a plethora of choice. The larger hotels generally have rather tranquil lounges. Many of the smaller pub/café style places have good, basic Canadian food, like wings and burgers, for under $10.

You may want to walk over to the new *Brew Pub* for a thin crust pizza before visiting one of the night-clubs. While all the night-clubs are quite busy during high season, the young locals seem to enjoy *Garfinkel's*. This is also a good choice for singles who may find most hotel and restaurant guests are already paired up. Of course in high season the whole resort is so busy that most drinking establishments will be doing good business.

Those who have are self-catering can find provisions easily, though those from your local supermarket are likely to be somewhat less expensive. Whistler has several liquor and cold beer stores so a night in with the gang is easy. Regardless of where you choose to stay at Whistler the entire area has been developed as a resort so there's lots to do and the staff are generally very helpful and friendly. Perhaps the only social drawback is the sometimes aloof and snobby clientele.

Other activities
If you ever tire of skiing, eating, drinking and generally having a good time ask at your hotel or pick up a copy of *Whistler Journal* for other ideas; the journal is free and is widely available. Heli-skiing is a bargain at $430 for 8,000-10,000ft of vertical in one day! There is horse-back riding, snowshoeing, swimming, skating, movies and massages! Your money will run out before the options do.

Vancouver Island

Telling Canadians suffering through a particularly harsh winter that Canada's warmest area can also have some excellent skiing is not the wisest form of diplomacy. At least everyone else can find some solace in the knowledge that while it is snowing heavily in the mountains rain is probably pouring down on the blossoming flowers in Victoria.

Vancouver Island is the largest island off the west coast of Canada and is the only area in the west that drops below the 49th parallel. However, staunchly 'British' Victoria is culturally very distant from the nearby USA. With the exception of the many coastal towns and beach areas, much of the island is remote or protected wilderness with a beautiful chain of mountains running down the middle.

Getting around the island
Driving is easy with the Trans-Canada running along the eastern shore and smaller routes branching out. A pleasant 1½ hour ferry trip brings you to the island though boats are much less frequent during winter (October to May). Ferries leave from Tsawassen, south of Vancouver, and Horseshoe Bay which is to the north and arrive at Swartz Bay and Nanimo respectively. A one-way trip costs around $27 with car and the boats generally run on time. Another ferry leaves from Powell River and goes to Comox. For further details contact **BC Ferries** (☎ 1-888-223-3779).

Skiing the island
As the island's largest resort points out, 'Where else can you ski and snowboard on a Pacific island?' (At least during New Zealand's summer!).

Mt Washington, in the middle of the island, is the largest and best known resort. However there are three other smaller resorts that are popular with locals: **Mount Cain**

(☎ 604-949-6997), up in the far north of the island close to Port McNeill, sometimes has heavy snowfalls; **Mount Arrowsmith** (☎ 604-723-7899) which is near Port Alberni; and further down the island near Courtney is **Forbidden Plateau** with 300m of vertical, one double chair and two T-bars, and 15 runs. A day ticket here is $16. For further details phone **Comox Valley Visitor Information Centre** (☎ 250-334-3234).

MT WASHINGTON

Mt Washington is a significant and expanding resort offering some of the best skiing on the west coast. Along with the superb skiing, the views on a clear day are some of the best of any resort in Canada. Perhaps the most outstanding feature of this resort is the copious snowfall – the average being 800cm (26ft) annually. During the 1994/95 season Washington had 22m of snow fall – that's over 70ft of white gold. The snow makes the trip up the hill worth the effort of putting the obligatory chains on your tires.

The skiing at Mt Washington can change at any moment as a result of snowfall – if you arrive to bald slopes in high season, just wait a day or two and you may be skiing powder. Undoubtedly the island has some of the heaviest and wettest snow in western Canada so it's a good idea to make sure your skis are well waxed and your legs in shape!

While there are plans for a second quad, Sunrise is the only one for the moment; however it offers good access to some intermediate and advanced runs along with some beautiful, powdery glades. The middle of the mountain, off the Whiskey Jack chair, is the domain of intermediates. When you're ready for something a bit steeper and less groomed head for the Powder Face.

Beginners are pretty much left near the bottom, but if you're just learning to ski and tired of falling, take a break by laughing at the tubers who are definitely much wetter than you at the end of the day!

Snowboarding

Washington is a good spot for boarders with all the powder, trees and glades, but to top it off there is a full snowboard park off the Whiskey Jack chair replete with pipes, table tops and all the toys. The powdery snow helps to cushion the less artistic landings.

Cross country

Mt Washington has 40km of groomed and set trails reaching out from the resort. Skiing in the area is a beautiful way of having a look at BC's oldest provincial park. A first-time lesson (1½ hrs), equipment and a trail pass costs $30. Day passes on their own cost $10.15.

❏ MT WASHINGTON
Base elevation: 1,105m (3,625ft)
Summit: 1,588m (5,215ft)
Vertical: 505m (1,657ft)
Lifts: 1 quad, 2 triples, 2 doubles, 2 surface and 1 tube
42 runs: 20% beginner, 45% intermediate, 35% advanced
Average snowfall: 800cm (26ft)

Contacts
Information and reservations: ☎ 250-338-1386
Snow phone: ☎ 250-338-1515, or ☎ 250-385-4636 (Vancouver)
Alpine Accommodations: ☎ 1-888-837-4663
Mt Washington Accommodations: ☎ 1-800-699-6499
Home page: www.vquest.com/alpine

Mt Washington

Lessons and rentals

Discover Skiing guaranteed packages with equipment and lift tickets are only $36.23 per day (the guarantee is that you will learn to ski!). The introductory snowboarding version costs $54.

Basic day rentals and group and private lessons for all levels are also available.

Lift tickets

	Adult	Youth (13-18)/Senior (65+)	Child (7-12)
Full day	$36.32	$28.90	$20.06

The High Five Pass – a package of five non-transferable day lift tickets – costs $163 for an adult. Children aged 6 and under ski free.

The price of the lift ticket and the High Five Pass does not include the BC road improvement levy, the cost of renting chains to climb up to the hill or the usual taxes, so count on another $20 or so per vehicle.

Getting there and around

From the lower mainland the fastest route to Mt Washington is via Nanaimo. From there the Comox Valley is 100km along good roads. The ski area is 25km west of the valley via the Strathcona Parkway. Excellent winter tires and/or chains are needed for the 16km from the base to the hill; these can be rented from the shop at the start of the access road.

Accommodation

The first hotel to be built in the village, the *Deer Lodge* (☎ 250-338-1386), has just been finished. Dozens of private chalets and condos are available for between $75 and $200.

For further information contact either **Alpine Accommodations** (☎ 1-888-837-4663 or **Mt Washington Accommodations** (☎ 1-800-699-6499).

Après ski

The resort is constantly expanding and thus becoming livelier, but at the time of writing there are only a couple of cafeterias and restaurants. *Fat Ted's Bar and Grill* has live music and it won't be long before other places offer evening entertainment.

The Okanagan

This area of central southern BC has long been popular with retirees as well as vacationers from both the lower mainland and Alberta. Unique in Canada, this is a major wine producing area set among arid hills while surrounded by snow-covered mountains. Certainly its beautiful lakes and surprisingly hot summer weather can take most of the credit for the region's continual expansion, however few can deny that as a winter destination the Okanagan is deservedly gaining acclaim.

The appeal to skiers is ever-growing and very understandable as all the ski areas tend to be warmer than those in the Rockies and the snowfalls are consistent and fairly generous. The base of the valley along which the Okanagan's cities and towns are spread has milder winters and the good roads commonly remain clear through the winter months. The resorts themselves are bent on expansion, offering ever more skiable terrain along with upgraded lift systems and enlarged base villages. Within the realm of the valley's ski fields, four resorts fit into the large category and each is worthy of attention.

Perhaps the only drawback from a skier's point of view is the views themselves! The central ranges are attractive in their own right though they are much more rounded than the dramatic Rocky Mountain crags or the towering coastal mountains. The major resorts are still on large mountains with the skiing environment being very different to that of the dry valley.

Location
It is generally accepted that the Okanagan region starts around the city of Kamloops at the junction of the Trans-Canada and the Yellowhead Highways and extends south through the cities of Vernon, Kelowna, Penticton and finally Osoyoos near the US border where the American Okanagan continues into the middle of Washington State. The valley is roughly 400 kilometres from the west coast.

Getting there and around
Due to the super Coquihalla highway ($10 toll), the Okanagan can be reached from the lower mainland within four hours, however good tires and/or chains are highly recommended as winter conditions can be treacherous. Taking the Trans-Canada through Fraser Canyon and Hope Princeton via Manning Park is an option depending on your destination, but you're still likely to need good tires/chains. A six to seven-hour drive is realistic along the Trans-Canada from southern Alberta.

SUN PEAKS RESORT
One of BC's most up-and-coming resorts, Sun Peaks at Tod Mountain has long been the local ski area for the people of Kamloops, a city at the northern end of the Okanagan. Since being bought by a Japanese firm and taken on by Canada's beloved Nancy Greene (former Olympic champion, currently Director of Skiing here) as its spokesperson, Sun Peaks' $150 million expansion has turned Tod Mountain into an international resort. Part of the appeal of Sun Peaks, aside from the three quads and 61 runs, is the village that is emerging from almost nothing. As a result of good planning and initiative Sun Peaks now has an abundance of ski in/ski out accommodation.

Now that Sun Peaks has an extensive lift system with two distinct access points to the village the good variety of terrain is almost always easy to get to. The runs at Sun Peaks are generally easy to follow and a quick look at the trail map will let you know where to head, based on your ability. For good beginners and intermediates who prefer skiing to sitting, the Sundance Express high-speed quad provides access to good, non-expert terrain. If you are really happy here, a separate and less expensive lift ticket (see Lift tickets) can be purchased. Intermediates who are getting used to deeper snow may enjoy the West Bowl T-bar at the top of the mountain, though it's only open weekends and holidays.

❏ SUN PEAKS
Base elevation: 1,198m (3,930ft)
Summit: 2,080m (6,824ft)
Vertical: 882m (2,894ft)
Lifts: 3 quads, 1 triple, 2 surface
61 runs: 24% beginner, 54% intermediate, 22% expert
Average snowfall: 450cm (177in)

Contacts
Information and reservations: ☎ 250-578-7842
Snow phone: ☎ 250-578-7232 (Kamloops), ☎ 604-290-0754 (Vancouver)
Accommodation reservations: ☎ 1-800-807-3257
Home page: www.sunpeaksresort.com

There is always a component of the expert set that needs to ski chutes, fortunately these can be accessed from the Crystal chair. Beginners can also use the Crystal chair in order to take the Five-Mile run. However they should be aware of speedsters emerging towards the bottom.

Snowboarding

As is true almost everywhere, there are probably more young people on boards than skis. As a result, Sun Peaks has constructed a 2500ft long snowboard park. The snow can be a little thin for boards on a few runs, but the park is always well maintained.

Cross country

Groomed and set tracks weave out from the village.

Lessons and rentals

Sun Peaks has joined the push to introduce skiing to as many people as possible and, with the presence of Nancy Greene, has managed to become an excellent place to learn. The basic $1^1/_2$ hour group lesson for all abilities costs $27. First timers can have three hours of instruction and lunch for $39. Private lessons start from $45/hour and advanced clinics are $35.

If you rent equipment in conjunction with lessons skis cost between $12 and $16. Boards can be rented for $18.50. Performance skis are cheap at $18.50 per day, boots are extra.

Lift tickets

	Adult	Youth (13-18)	Child (6-12)	Senior (65+)
Full Day (per day for 1-2 days)	$41	$36	$23	$27
Full day (per day for 3+ days)	$38	$24	$21	$33
Sundance Express only	$29	$25	$16	$19

All sorts of ski-and-stay packages are available from $69+ tax per night including lift and accommodation based on double occupancy.

Getting there and around

Much like the whole of the Okanagan, Kamloops has become progressively easier to get to. Traditionally the junction of Canada's two major railways, Kamloops is also the point at which the Trans-Canada meets the more northern Yellowhead highway. There are now three routes one can take between Kamloops and Vancouver: the beautiful Fraser Valley along the Trans-Canada, the new faster Coquihalla route, or the long way around on highway #99 via Whistler. Vancouver is a $4^1/_4$ hour drive while Calgary is over seven hours.

Sun Peaks is 50km north of Kamloops off the #5 north. As Kamloops is a fairsized city there are many bus options and the train through Fraser Canyon is always popular. Kamloops also has an airport – the resort offers pick up from the airport.

Since Sun Peaks is within a couple of hours of the other ski destinations in the Okanagan, it can easily be included as part of a ski trip to the other resorts.

Accommodation and après ski

Sun Peaks' ever-expanding community is divided between the village and the smaller Burfield Base area; all bookings can be made through the reservations office (☎ 1-800-807-3257).

Sun Peaks Resort

Among the six hotels are Nancy Greene's *Cahilty Lodge* (☎ 1-800-244-8424), the *Sheraton Sundance Lodge* (☎ 1-800-483-2888) and a brand new *Radisson* hotel (☎ 1-800-333-3333). Many other hotels and chalets are available. Hotel prices start from $120 for doubles and rise quickly, although there are some well-priced condo units very close to the lifts. Unfortunately there is as yet no budget accommodation.

The four Day Lodges all serve food and the new hotels have good restaurants; the resort also has the requisite pubs and cafés. Live music is common.

Remember this is ranching country so steak is a staple part of the diet. It's well worth trying some local wine and the BC salmon is generally fresh. One can expect a great deal more growth at this resort over the years.

SILVER STAR

Close to the city of Vernon, Silver Star is an excellent family destination with lots of snow, a good lift system and a very attractive and compact village. The village is situated a third of the way up the front face and is therefore completely accessible on skis. Part of the pleasure of skiing at Silver Star, aside from the mountain itself, is the friendly and professional way the whole resort is run. The staff are helpful and the small village seems to have all the necessities, without much duplication.

Silver Star often provides some great powder and when it is a little bare in the fall and spring you'll find yourself slipping over grass instead of rocks! It is relatively easy to figure out where you want to ski based on your ability. Vance Creek (the south face) where you arrive at the village is dominated by beginner and intermediate runs, whereas Putnam Creek (the north face) has advanced and expert terrain. Beginners have a couple of T-bars to choose from and an area off the Silver Queen chair where you shouldn't get caught up with the experts. There is also a small area with night skiing.

While Silver Star is not huge in area, the 84 runs offer almost all possible challenges and the runs are long enough to please all standards. Feedback from people on the lifts seems to suggest that this resort pleases everyone – many return year after year.

Cross country

There are 35 kilometres of track – four kilometres of which are lit at night! Tickets cost $10 per day, or $8 per day for multi-day passes. Just down the road there are another 50km of park-maintained tracks at Sovereign Lake. A $12 pass covers both areas.

Snowboarding

Of course! There is a park on the front side; a traditional half-pipe is linked to the park. The resort's family image attracts many young people.

❏ SILVER STAR
Base elevation: 1,133m (3,700ft)
Summit: 1,915m (6,280ft)
Vertical: 760m (5,250ft)
Lifts: 3 quads (2 detachable), 2 doubles, 3 surface
84 runs: 20% beginner, 50% intermediate, 30% advanced
Average snowfall: 570cm (18ft)
Lift operating hours: 8.30am-3.30pm, night skiing 3.30-9pm (depending on conditions)

Contacts
Information and reservations: ☎ 1-800-663-4431 or ☎ 250-542-0224
Snow phone: ☎ 250-542-1745
Ski school: ☎ 250-558-6065
Home page: www.silverstarmtn.com

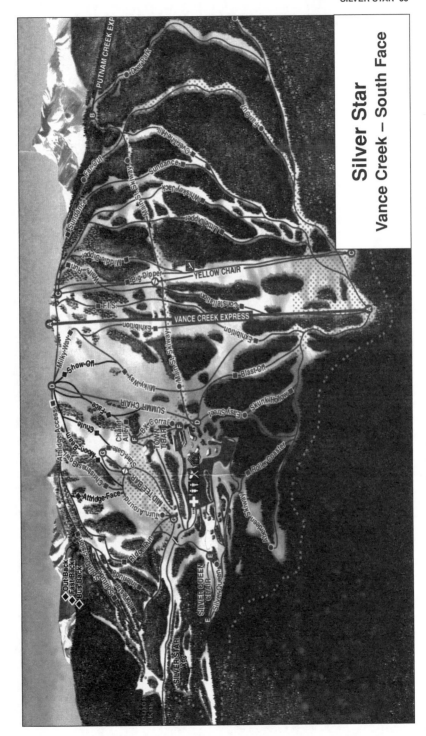

Silver Star
Vance Creek – South Face

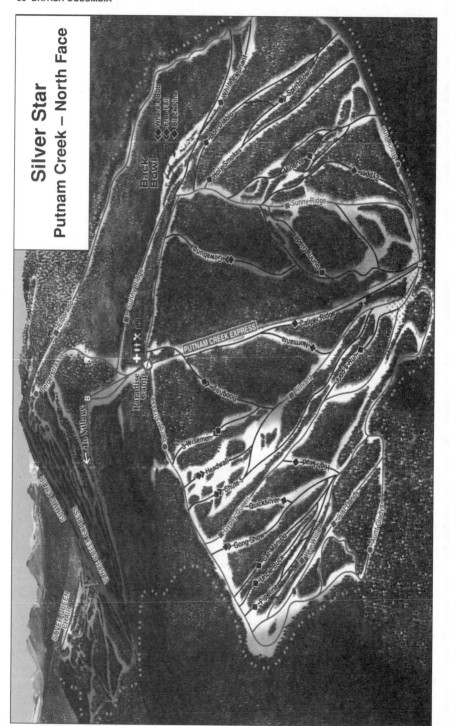

Silver Star
Putnam Creek – North Face

Lessons and rentals

Silver Star prides itself on its ski school (☎ 250-558-6065) and all accounts suggest this is fair. There is a myriad of lesson options with several multi-day programs. The school has some innovative techniques for teaching new boarders, including using different length poles for practising long, sweeping turns. This is a popular place for kids to learn how to ski and it is not uncommon to see whole schools having lessons on the mountain.

A five-day program for adults with 1½ hours of lessons daily and including lift tickets costs $275. The same program for teenagers but with more instruction costs $215, and for kids the price is $180.

Day rentals start from $26 for skis and $37 for boards; not surprisingly top quality equipment costs more. Five-day rentals represent good savings.

Lift tickets

	Adult	Youth (13-18)	Child (6-12)	Senior (65+)*
Full day	$45	$38	$23	$31

*Seniors aged over 70 and children aged 5 and under ski free.

Afternoon tickets start at 12.30pm. Rates decrease significantly for multi-day passes – a five-day adult ticket costs $175.

Getting there and around

The village is 20 kilometres (12 miles) east of the city of Vernon. The nearest airport is at Kelowna which is 45 minutes south of Vernon; a shuttle can be booked from the airport. As is true with many access roads, the last few kilometres up to the hill are often icy and attention must be given to the narrow bends.

Accommodation and après ski

The six village hotels are all central and comfortable with rooms to suit most needs though unfortunately not all wallets. Prices range from $105 to over $500. Most prices include a lift ticket and Silver Star does represent good value when compared to other large resorts. RV parking is available from $19 per night. For reservations phone ☎ 1-800-663-4431 or ☎ 250-542-0224.

For budget-oriented accommodation you'll need to drive down to Vernon where vacancies are easy to find during the winter months. It is also possible to rent privately owned condos – for details contact the information and reservations office.

The village may be small but there is a deli, a café, a dining room, an Italian restaurant and even a saloon! This is where you'll usually find a band and much of the young crowd. The entire resort seems to employ friendly staff and the food is good and reasonably priced. *Lord Aberdeen Hotel* houses a small store and liquor agency. There is not, as yet, a bank machine.

Quite often the resort holds talks about the area and other family-related activities. To find out what is happening pick up a copy of *Entertainment Weekly* when you arrive.

BIG WHITE

This is the largest ski area in the Okanagan, and the residents of the nearby wealthy city of Kelowna are thrilled by the mountain's continuous expansion. With over 100 runs and a high snow accumulation, Big White is well suited to most skiers. The resort's location in the middle of the Okanagan makes it accessible from many areas and the skiing environment is similar to the other resorts of this region. Big White's village area is expanding and more and more weekenders are building chalets there. The other real bonus for young skiers is the presence of budget beds, something unfortunately lacking in other areas.

Big White

If you're just driving up for the day don't bother going as far as the village as tickets can be purchased at the base of the Gem Lake Express quad. Experts and tree fans may enjoy skiing here so much that they won't want to go anywhere else. Beginners should head for the Bullet Express and up the Alpine T-bar if their legs aren't too tired.

❏ BIG WHITE
Base elevation: 1,504m (7,500ft)
Summit: 3,318m (7,606ft)
Vertical: 777m (2,550ft)
Lifts: 5 quads (4 high-speed), 1 triple, 1 double, 2 surface
100+ runs and glades: 18% beginner, 56% intermediate, 26% advanced
Average snowfall: 750cm (24.5ft)
Lift operating hours: 9am-3.30pm midweek; 8.30am-3.30pm weekends;
night skiing Tuesday to Saturday from mid-December to early April 3.30-9pm.

Contacts
Information: ☎ 1-800-663-2772 or ☎ 250-765-3101
Reservations: ☎ 250-765-8888
Snow phone: ☎ 250-765-7669
Home page: www.bigwhite.com

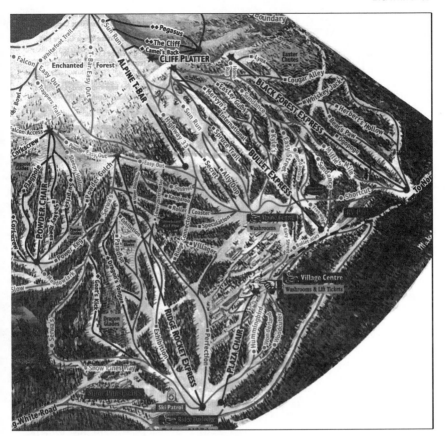

For new skiers and boarders who are beyond the very basic stages of their chosen sport, Big White is a good choice as you won't be stuck on some small lift at the bottom. Almost the entire mountain is accessible to most abilities and you can still generally avoid the faster skiers. Those who happen to enjoy bowls with double-black chutes may want to try the Alpine T-bar, though the runs are not terribly long. The other great areas for advanced skiers are Big White's glades – have a taste off the Powder chair. Intermediates have the rest of the mountain with the greatest variety off the Ridge Rocket and Black Forest quads.

Snowboarding
Big White has eight acres of snowboarding in two parks with a half-pipe off the Ridge Rocket and a terrain park near the bottom of the Bullet Express. Except for those boarders who just love speed it would seem that Big White's extensive glades are by far the best fun for those who are at one with their boards – check the snow conditions first!

Cross country
Twenty five kilometres of nordic trails can be skied to from the village, just keep going past the base of the Black Forest Express.

Lessons and rentals

Big White has 80 ski pros and package options for all ages and abilities. Perhaps the most complete package is the family ski week with lessons, wine and family entertainment. An adult five-day lift pass, lesson and rental package goes for $363.

Skis can be rented from $20; a group lesson also costs about $20.

Lift tickets

	Adult	Youth (13-18)	Junior (6-12)	Senior (65+)*
One Day	$46	$38	$24	$33

*Seniors over 70 ski free, as do children aged 5 and under.

A five-day ticket (adult, $205) is good value, though the best deals include accommodation and perhaps lessons.

Getting there and around

Big White is 45 minutes east of Kelowna so you can get there in less than an hour from the airport. Kelowna is a 45-minute flight from Vancouver. A free shuttle is available – call the reservations office (☎ 250-765-8888) in advance.

If driving, watch for the sign to turn off highway #33. While the access road is not particularly steep it can still be extremely slippery.

Accommodation and après ski

Big White has a very attractive village area with a large hotel, many condo and chalet options and two hostels: *Hostelling International* (☎ 250-765-7050) is at the top of the village and has beds from $17, *Bumps* is a private hostel starting from $15 for dorms.

The principal hotel is the very attractive *White Crystal Inn* (☎ 250-765-4611), doubles are around $180 during regular season but it is always worth asking about deals. All sorts of different condos can be rented, most with ski in/ski out. Prices vary significantly. For accommodation inquiries (apart from the hostels) call the Reservations office (☎ 250-765-888 or ☎ 1-800-663-2772).

Big White's village is self contained with a reasonable selection of restaurants, cafés and bars. If you decide to stay during a holiday period there is plenty of live entertainment at the two main saloons. There is as yet no bank machine, but the small shops offer Interact so bank card holders can get cash; everyone takes credit cards. However, if you're planning to stay at Big White for some time it may be worth stocking up on some of the basics in Kelowna.

Kelowna has plenty of affordable accommodation with many major Canadian hotel chains and conference-style hotels that are fairly quiet over winter. This is a good choice if you're looking for a base from which to explore the whole of the Okanagan. Kelowna also has a great variety of restaurants and the best collection of BC wines.

APEX MOUNTAIN RESORT

The most southerly of the Okanagan's major resorts, Apex is an attractive mountain with some exhilarating steep runs and among the best lift prices in Canada. It's associated with the small city of **Penticton** which is a mecca during the summer for young Albertans who flock in for the beaches and parties. Some of the fun seems to spill over to the pubs up in Apex's small mountain village. Again, the drives are reasonable enough that Apex can be enjoyed while visiting other mountains in the Okanagan, though it's probably worth staying nearby for a couple of days.

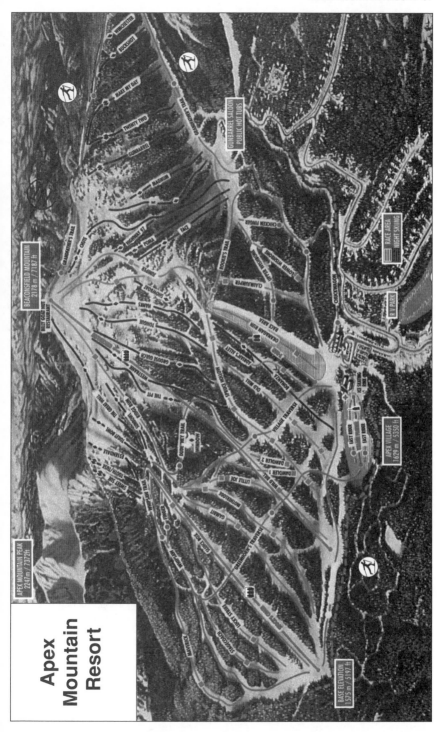

Apex Mountain Resort

There's only one way to the top of the mountain and it's a bastion for advanced skiers. Beginners might get a little tired of the one green run from the top, however the triple stock chair is long enough to provide decent entertainment for green and blue fans. From the summit there are a few good long intermediate runs which also offer a bit of relief from the moguls. There are also a number of good chutes for those who love the steep double blacks. As Apex has some long steep runs it is on the racing circuit so it is not uncommon to see young teams from other hills running gates.

Night skiing is available off the T-bar, which is just long enough to make a bit of after dinner exercise worthwhile.

Snowboarding
The trees tend to be a bit tight and the ski-out from the serious black runs can be a little long, but on powder days Apex is always good fun.

Cross country
Apex has 12 kilometres just off the village including a one kilometre night-lit loop – skiing here is free.

Six kilometres away at the **Nickel Plate Nordic Centre** there are another 50km of track, 30km of which are groomed for skating – the other 20km are back-country trails. There is no formal charge to ski here but a donation is required.

Lessons and rentals
Discover Skiing packages start from $30 for adults ($27 for teens) and the snowboard version is $40 ($37 for teens); the package includes a lesson, rental equipment and a Poma lift ticket.

Equipment and lift ticket ski packages start from $59 for adults ($45 for teens); the equivalent packages for snowboarders are $69 for adults and $55 for teens – prices given are per day.

Kids' packages, which include a group lesson and time at the Kids Club, are available for $39 for a full day and $29 for a half day.

Group lessons cost $27 for 1½ hours (if two or more lessons are booked the rate is reduced to $24); a private lesson is $44.

Lift tickets

	Adult (13-64)	Junior(8-12)/Senior (65+)	Child (7 and under)
Full Day	$33	$24	Free

❏ APEX MOUNTAIN
Base elevation: 1,575m (5,075ft)
Summit: 2,178m (7,187ft)
Vertical: 605m (2,000ft)
Lifts: 1 quad, 1 triple, 2 surface
56 runs: 16% beginner, 48% intermediate, 36% advanced
Average snowfall: N/A (however accumulations appear comparable to other resorts in the area)
Lift operating hours: 9am-3.30pm; night skiing 6-9.30pm Friday and Saturday and nightly during the Christmas/New Year and Spring holidays.

Contacts
Information and reservations: ☎ 1-800-387-2739 or ☎ 250-292-8111 or ☎ 250-492-2880
Home page: www.apexresort.com

Getting there and around

Depending on how fast you drive, Apex is about 45 minutes west of Penticton along Green Mountain Rd. The route is marked at the junction in Penticton and again at the turn before heading up the fairly steep mountain. However, between the two you pass through Native Indian land and the No Trespassing/Private Road signs can be somewhat disconcerting. At the beginning of the 1997/98 season there was some conflict over the road which saw it closed for a period of time but all is now fine, though one should drive within the limits as a respect to the First Nation's owners.

Transport can be arranged from Penticton. Kelowna and its airport are less than one hour north and Vancouver is 400 kilometres away. As a note of caution, the Apex access road is well maintained though quite steep and it can have large accumulations even if the valley is bare. As a result it can be slippery if you drive up before the gravel truck. Everything in the tiny village is within easy walking distance.

Accommodation and après ski

Apex can provide great deals. The attractive *Inn at Apex* (☎ 1-800-387-2739) at the base of the mountain has a significant variety of package deals which can come as affordably as $49 for one night and one day of skiing, midweek.

Apex also has an RV (motor home) Park with $15 hook-up rates and a variety of condos to choose from.

Penticton has almost unlimited accommodation options during the winter.

At the village there is one dining room, a café, a cafeteria and a couple of bars including the lively *Gunbarrel Saloon & Restaurant* which closes at 2am.

OTHER RESORTS IN THE OKANAGAN

Harper Mountain

This is a smaller mountain about 1/2 hour north of Kamloops along the #5. The valley in which it lies has good snow and the mountain has one triple chair and one T-bar serving 25 runs and over 400m. There are also eight kilometres of cross-country trails nearby.

The chair doesn't open until 12.30pm on weekdays and lift tickets cost $19 for adults during the week and $24 on weekends. For information and reservations phone ☎ 250-372-2119.

There is also some skiing 1 1/2 hours up the Yellowhead at Clearwater.

Crystal Mountain

This small, friendly ski area is up above **Westbank**, 25 minutes south of Kelowna. Crystal has 200 vertical metres, a double chair and three surface lifts. It's a steep but well maintained drive to the base. For information and reservations phone ☎ 250-768-5189.

Mount Baldy

Close to the American border, at the far south of the Okanagan, Mount Baldy is only six kilometres from Penticton airport and 37km from **Oliver**. There are only two surface lifts, but high snowfalls, good trees and glades. There are also 16km of cross-country close by. For information and reservations phone ☎ 250-446-2424.

Phoenix Mountain

This small family resort just outside Grand Forks in southern BC is between the Okanagan and the Kootenays. Phoenix is a friendly place with two surface lifts and nine runs. There is also a good selection of cross country nearby. For information and reservations phone ☎ 250-442-2813.

The Kootenays

The Kootenays, or Kootenay Country, has become a bit of a generic term to denote the southern mountainous region of British Columbia. From Kootenay National Park along the BC-Alberta/Banff boundary to the Okanagan, this aboriginal word has been given to this snowy, lake-filled region. The southern part of the Kootenays has long been a popular summer vacation spot and is an ideal skiing area for everyone, particularly Americans heading north.

Roads in the region are good, but heavy snowfalls and winter storms can leave them closed from time to time. Cranbrook in the Columbia Valley has an airport as does Castlegar further west. Driving from either Vancouver or Calgary is fairly easy but rather time consuming. BC's Kootenay Country makes a great add-on to a trip down the Rocky Mountain Trench, or from the Okanagan. The hot springs at **Nakusp** and **Ainsworth** make any trip worthwhile.

Rossland and **Nelson** in the southern part of the Kootenays are popular centres for skiing and also for hippies because of the alternative culture that has developed in the towns. The many valleys are beautiful and the communities interesting and diverse.

Skiing the Kootenays

All summer, people in the Kootenays golf, boat or hike, but come winter everything revolves around the tons of snow that fall on the area! Cross country, back country and excellent alpine make the area an ideal winter playground. Trees and powder are the greatest draw for skiers and boarders. If you are a snowmobiler or serious back-country skier, this area is a major destination. However, remember that avalanches claim lives every year – all precautions must be taken.

Aside from Whitewater and Red Mountain – two great reasons to visit the south Kootenays – there are also minor hills at **Salmo** (☎ 604-357-2323), **Sparwood** (☎ 604-265-3312), and Nakusp.

RED MOUNTAIN

Located near the old mining town of Rossland, in the west Kootenays, Red is a great mountain but very remote. This is a bastion for experts and tree lovers with some of the best unpatrolled extreme skiing within Canada – and within area boundaries. Over the years some of the trees have been cleared out and some runs widened, however Red is still home to some of the best treed runs in Canada. The famous triple blacks are no longer marked, though double blacks abound. Plenty of unmarked extreme runs can be found, but be careful – Red acknowledges its 'rugged' nature and leaves you to ski at your own risk.

Red has some of the best skiing in BC and the whole mountain is worth exploring. Almost all the double blacks as well as some intermediate and even two beginner runs are reached from the Motherlode triple chair. The three other lifts cover the rest of the trails with only the T-bar not accessing advanced runs. While locals certainly learn to ski on Red, this is probably not the mountain for novice skiers. The true beginner is just as comfortable here as anywhere else, but a lot of confidence is required before venturing further up the mountain.

❏ **RED MOUNTAIN**
Base elevation: 1,190m (3,800ft)
Summit: 2,040m (6,700ft)
Vertical: 850m (2,800ft)
Lifts: 3 triple, 1 double, 1 surface
83 runs (including groomed and ungroomed): 10% beginner, 45% intermediate, 45% advanced
Average snowfall: 762cm (6ft 5in)

Contacts
Information and reservations: ☎ 1-800-663-0105 or ☎ 250-362-7700 or ☎ 250-362-7384
24hr snow phone: ☎ 250-362-5500
Ski school: ☎ 250-362-7115 or the toll free reservations number above

The double chair is separate from the rest of the mountain and is a good place to warm up on some shorter, but still challenging, runs. There is now a more extensive system of easy runs, and good intermediate ones have helped to open the mountain to everyone. Tree fans will still be thrilled almost everywhere. There are plans to open another peak with a couple of new chairs – this should result in more of the same. Great!

Snowboarding
It's only recently that snowboarders have been welcomed here – not surprisingly this comes as a great relief to local fans. With nearly eight metres of snow and plenty of chutes to jump down this is a natural place for boarders to test themselves.

Cross country
The Blackjack cross-country area just across from Red has 50km of track and it also offers many more fantastic back-country opportunities.

Lessons and rentals
Two-hour group lessons are $25. Lift, lesson and rental packages are $51 per day or $39 for the beginner package.

Ski rental packages on their own cost an adult $25 (child $17), or $31 (child $24) for a snowboard package.

Lift tickets

	Adult	Student (13-18)	Senior (65+)	Junior (7-12)
Full Day	$39	$32	$28	$20

Children aged 6 and under ski free.

Getting there and around
It's worth going to Red for a few days as it is a bit of a journey from most major centres. The slopes are four kilometres uphill from the old mining town of Rossland which is 10km uphill from the larger community of **Trail**. Unfortunately the whole area is a full day from either Calgary or Vancouver. However, as it's located near the Washington border, Spokane is only 2½ hours south. Greyhound runs a service to Rossland. Red is also close to Nelson and Whitewater so hippies and powder fans can easily kill a season in the area.

Accommodation and après ski
Right at the base of the slopes are a few small hotels; more are being built. For rooms on site, or in the area, you can phone the reservations office (☎ 1-800-663-0105).

Red Mountain

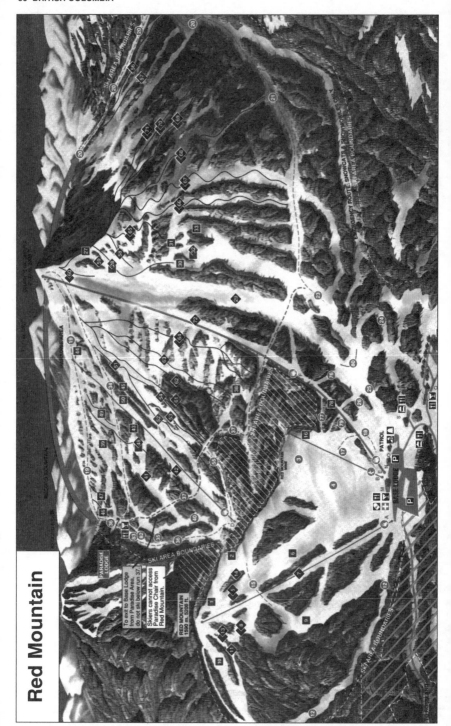

PARADISE LODGE

To exit to Base Lodge
from Paradise Area,
do not ski below run 37.

Skiers cannot access
Paradise Chair from
Red Mountain.

RED MOUNTAIN
1590 m. 5200 ft.

PATROL

TRAILS – RED MOUNTAIN
- ● 3 T-Bar Slope
- ● 4 Ski School Alley 'Go Slow'
- ● 12 Dale's Trail
- ● 15 Tower 10 Cat Track
- ● 17 Little Red Run
- ● 18 Granite Access
- ■ 1 Upper Back Trail
- ■ 2 Lower Back Trail
- ■ 6 Face of Red
- ■ 9 Lower War Eagle
- ■ 10 Sally's Alley (to Dale's Trail)
- ■ 16 Big Red Run
- ◆ 7 Towers of Red
- ◆ 11 Poochie's Cabin Run (to Dale's)
- ◆ 14 Stilhang
- ◆ 5 The Cliff
- ◆◆ 8 Upper War Eagle
- ◆◆ 13 Hole in the Wall

TRAILS – GRANITE MOUNTAIN
- ● 19 Ridge Road
- ● 20 Long Squaw
- ● 21 Easy Street
- ● 23 Indian Flats
- ● 24 Corky's Road
- ● 25 Corky's Field
- ● 26 Tower 3 Breakover
- ● 34 Boardwalk
- ● 35 Silver Sheep Sneak
- ● 36 Silver Sheep
- ● 37 Southside Road
- ● 40 Sour Dough Alley
- ● 55 Ledges Traverse
- ● 76 Panhandle
- ● 77 Zig Zag

TRAILS – GRANITE MOUNTAIN (CONT)
- ● 79 Colt
- ● 80 Corky's Traverse
- ● 81 Stagger By
- ● 82 Buckeye
- ● 83 Badger
- ● 27 Buffalo Ridge
- ■ 30 Tom's Run
- ■ 31 Boutry Cat Track
- ■ 33 Jake's Slope
- ■ 38 Shortcuts
- ■ 39 Southern Comfort
- ■ 43 Gambler
- ■ 44 Southern Belle Traverse
- ■ 45 Southern Belle
- ■ 46 Mini Bowls
- ■ 47 Meadows
- ■ 49 Ruby Monday
- ■ 50 Inagadadavida
- ■ 78 Sluice
- ●■ 28 Main Run
- ●■ 32 Schuss
- ●■ 48 Maggie's Farm
- ◆ 29 Granite Towers
- ◆ 41 Ruby Tuesday
- ◆ 42 Gambler Towers
- ◆ 51 Jumbo Traverse
- ◆ 52 Ledges
- ◆ 53 Alder Gully
- ◆ 54 Jumbo
- ◆ 56 Beer Belly
- ◆ 57 Doug's Run
- ◆ 58 Shoulder
- ◆ 59 Papoose Bowl
- ◆ 61 Han's Run
- ◆ 62 The Orchards

TRAILS – GRANITE MOUNTAIN (CONT)
- ◆ 63 Powder Fields
- ◆ 72 Centre Star
- ◆ 60 Link's Run
- ◆ 64 Pale Face
- ◆ 65 1st Slide
- ◆ 66 2nd Slide
- ◆ 67 3rd Slide
- ◆ 68 Roots
- ◆ 69 Cambodia
- ◆ 70 Needles
- ◆ 71 Short Squaw

LIFTS
- **A** Red chairlift
- **B** T Bar
- **D** Paradise triple chairlift
- **E** Silverlode triple chairlift
- **F** Motherlode triple chairlift

At the base, *Ram's Head Inn* (☎ 250-362-9577) is a nice no-smoking hotel with doubles from $94 per person including lift ticket and breakfast. There is also the small *Red Shutter Inn* (☎ 250-362-5131). Many different packages are available.

The 42-bed international *Mountain Shadow Hostel* (☎ 250-362-7160) in Rossland has beds from $17 per night. Located between Rossland and Red mountain is *Rossland Motel* (☎ 250-362-7218) – the amenities include kitchen units, a sauna, and a wax room to fix up your skis. Doubles start at a reasonable $50.

Certainly in Rossland and further on in Trail there are plenty of other hotels and motels which are generally cheaper than the major resorts.

Red has two lodges with food and the *Gamblers Retreat Restaurant* at the base. Rossland has several restaurants and pubs – while the town has not yet become as fashionable as Nelson, cafés and vegetarian menus are slowly appearing.

WHITEWATER

Just outside the groovy town of Nelson, Whitewater is known for its extremely generous snowfalls which have made this resort a haven for real powder fans. Other advantages are that skiers don't generally have to endure lift lines and that this compact resort offers a good diversity of runs, from bowls to trees.

Part of the appeal of Whitewater is the region – with Nelson just down the road and Red Mountain not too far away, skiers can stay entertained all season. Furthermore, cross-country skiers simply can't run out of back-country options. Another bonus to the south Kootenays is cost. Generally ski packages are less expensive here than at major resorts. Perhaps the only drawback to the area is its location – the closest significant centre being Spokane. With the heavy snowfalls roads can close with alarming regularity.

Most of the skiing terrain in essentially covered by two double chairs. Powder is generally found everywhere. Advanced skiers want to head for the two bowls off the Summit chair, and perhaps into the large treed cliff area. Beginners and intermediates will have fun off the Silver King chair and remember – falling in powder hurts less.

Snowboarding
With the heavy snowfalls there are just as many boarders as skiers.

Cross country
There are no groomed runs at the hill, but the area has cross-country centres and back-country opportunities abound.

❏ WHITEWATER
Base elevation: 1,640m (5,400ft)
Summit: 2,040m (6,700ft)
Vertical: 396m (1,300ft)
Lifts: 2 doubles, 1 surface
Runs: 20% beginner, 40% intermediate, 40% advanced
Average snowfall: 1,000 cm (34ft)
Lift operating hours: 9am-3.30pm

Contacts
Information and reservations: ☎ 1-800-666-9420 or ☎ 250-354-4944
24hr snow phone: ☎ 250-352-7669
Home page: www.skiwhitewater.com

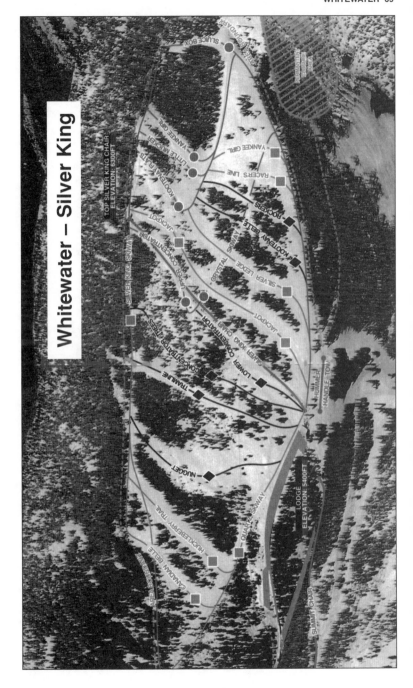

Whitewater – Silver King

Whitewater – Summit

Lessons and rentals
Whitewater has the full range of services, although with the restrictions of a smaller resort.

Lift tickets

	Adult	Youth (13-18*)/senior (65+)	Junior (7-12)
Full day	$35	$27	$21

* Students with ID are also entitled to the youth reduction. Children aged 6 and under ski free.

Getting there and around
The problem for Nelson is that it is a good distance from most major centres with Spokane, Washington being a three-hour drive. Nelson is nestled on the coast of Kootenay Lake in south central BC at the junction of #3 and #6 highways. Vancouver and Calgary are eight hours either way.

Accommodation and après ski
There is no accommodation right at the hill but Nelson is just a few kilometres west and there is an abundance of good, affordable shelter offering all sorts of package deals associated with Whitewater. Reservations (☎ 1-800-666-9420) can organise ski-and-stay packages in Nelson for as little as $50 a day. Obviously the accommodation is basic, but Nelson isn't really a town for the upwardly mobile. It will be interesting to see whether it is 'discovered' in the next 20 years.

The ski area has a small lodge, but Nelson is full of action. Aside from the many small town pubs, there are several progressive cafés and good restaurants, including some vegetarian ones! It's difficult to get lost and the friendly locals will give you any information you need.

The Rocky Mountain Trench

This stunning, wide valley forms the western boundary of the Rockies and is often referred to as the Radium or Columbia Valley. The Trench begins in central BC, west of Mount Robson, and continues south into the United States. It marks the divide between the Rockies and the older Columbia mountains.

The southerly, most populated region of the Trench is between Golden and Cranbrook. The communities in this area are part of BC but they use Alberta's Mountain Time. Generally they have milder winters than the other valleys of the Rockies.

Two of the great pleasures of the Trench are the easily accessible hot springs at Radium and Fairmont as well as some harder to find pools around Kimberley. In addition, the generally dry valley makes travel painless and the well-equipped resorts and towns are worthy of a visit. The largest resort in the valley is Panorama and the most interesting town by far is the self-made Bavarian community of Kimberley.

From Banff and Calgary the Columbia Valley is easy to reach along the Kootenay Parkway. Turn south on route #93 from the Trans-Canada west of Banff to enter BC and Kootenay National Park. This drive is one of the most spectacular in the Rockies and back-country and cross-country fans don't even need to go all the way to Radium!

Skiing the Trench

The Trench can have exceptional, light powder and provides access to some of the world's best heli-skiing. Unfortunately, snowfalls at the resorts are not always as generous as you may hope for, but when Panorama or Kimberley receive a large dumping they can have some of the best skiing in BC. Fernie's consistently great snow means it is worth considering as part of a ski trip in the region, though technically it is not in the Trench.

WHITETOOTH

This is a small resort near the town of **Golden**, BC. Fortunately it is on the Trans-Canada highway and has some great skiing. Golden is located at the very top of the Columbia Valley and is a common spot to stop for the night when heading either east or west. For those who like skiing trees, or if you have a half day to kill, Whitetooth offers some good fun.

Although this is still a small resort it is well worth keeping an eye on its development. It seems foreign money is pouring in and the resort may well expand five-fold over the next few years. For the moment, Whitetooth is open only at weekends (Friday to Monday) but daily during the Christmas/New Year and BC Spring breaks. As a result the skiing is still very good and the conditions natural. There is a small T-bar for beginners and a double chair which provides access to the rest of the mountain – if expansions do continue, the glacier may become part of the skiable terrain.

Skiing is affordable and there is a small ski rental shop. Lessons are also available. Cross-country options abound in the area and the resort maintains 17km of trails. Golden is also a well known place for snowmobiling.

Getting there and around

The town of Golden is on the Trans-Canada one hour west of Lake Louise. The ski area (Whitetooth) is four kilometres from Golden. Since Golden is at the top of the Columbia Valley it is a good place to start a ski trip in the Trench.

From Calgary, Golden is a three-hour drive – be careful on the road east of Field, the exposed conditions make it icy.

Lift tickets

	Adult (19-59)	Youth (13-18)	Child (6-12)	Senior (60+)
Full day	$28	$20	$12	$20
Half day	$20	$15	$8	$15
T bar only	$12	$8	$8	$12

❏ WHITETOOTH
Base elevation: 1,311m (4,300ft)
Summit: 1,841m (6,040ft)
Vertical: 530m (1,740ft)
Lifts: 1 double, 1 surface
13 runs: 20% beginner, 30% intermediate, 50% advanced
Average snowfall: unknown

Contacts
For skiing information: ☎ 250-344-6114
For reservations: ☎ 1-800-622-4653
Home page: www.rockies.net/~whitetooth/

Whitetooth

TRAILS

- ● A Little Bend
- ● C Beaverfoot
- ● D Bugaboo
- ● F Blaeberry
- ● 1 Rotary Route
- ● 2 Trappers Trail
- ● 3 Mistaya
- ● 6 Big Bend
- ●◆ 4 Wapiti
- ●◆ 5 Nose Dive
- ●◆ 7 Wolverine
- ●◆ 9 Waitabit
- ■ B Crowfoot
- ■ E Mummery
- ■ 10 Glenogle

- ■ 11 Kinbasket
- ■◆ 15 Kicking Horse
- ◆ 8 Lynx
- ◆ 12 Grizzly
- ◆ 13 Porcupine
- ◆ 14 Pioneer
- ◆ 16 Race Run

LIFTS
Moberly T-Bar
Pioneer double chairlift

Accommodation

There are no rooms at the base of the hill, but Golden has a variety of accommodation. For reservations phone ☎ 1-800-622-4653.

PANORAMA

This is the largest ski area in the Rocky Mountain Trench and at 1,311m (4,300ft) Panorama is home to the second highest vertical in North America. Since being developed by Intrawest, the same group that is responsible for Whistler and Mont Tremblant, Panorama has developed into a significant resort with a wide variety of hill accommodation, featuring a lodge, hotels and condos with wonderful outdoor hot tubs to prepare you for the next day's skiing. The views are spectacular and with such a large vertical drop the conditions suit almost any skier.

Despite all the development, the resort retains its isolated feel and everyone staying at the hill is there to ski. While there are now a few restaurants and bars, the real story is the ever expanding terrain. Panorama still has long, challenging trails you can have all to yourself.

Panorama is predominantly for intermediate to advanced skiers – even the green runs are on the steeper side. The only real drawback can be the crusty snow, though the top tends to be a bit softer. Snowmaking tends to compensate for mother nature and the hi-tech grooming means the snow is as well prepared as humanly possible.

Despite its enormous size, the mountain is fairly easy to figure out based on ability, though the best runs without a doubt cover the entire east and west sides of the mountain. Once on Schober's Dream you must travel all the way to the base and it takes at least three lifts to start again from the top! Halfway down check out the glades – a fun area and a beautiful place for a picnic. This area is not recommended for beginners, although with a bit of work most people can enjoy it. On the other hand, the View of a Thousand Peaks on the eastern side has some serious double blacks. The Extreme Zone of this area may be the only place on the mountain with powder and the bowl is the steepest in the region. Watch for rocks lower down.

The lower third of the mountain is for beginners and intermediates and the runs are nice and long. The Horizon chair running up the middle is a bit slow, but the views are some of the best in Canada. This chair has good, well-groomed intermediate runs and a few with smaller bumps.

The Summit T-bar was a great addition several years ago. If you can handle some fairly steep runs, the views are worth the trip. Have a go if time or drop back into the Extreme Dream.

Perhaps it is because of the vertical, or the well-designed diverse runs, but either way almost all visitors to Panorama end up loving the mountain. Before heading to Panorama call and make sure all the runs you want are open – the snow is variable.

❏ PANORAMA

Base elevation: 1,158m (3,800ft)
Summit: 2,408m (7,900ft)
Vertical: 1,311m (4,300ft)
Lifts: 1 quad, 1 triple, 2 doubles, 3 surface
80+ runs and expanding: 20% beginner, 55% intermediate/advanced, 25% expert
Average snowfall: 266cm (105in) also 70% snowmaking
Lift operating hours: 9am-4pm

Contacts

Information and reservations: ☎ 1-800-663-2929 or ☎ 250-342-6941
Snow phone: ☎ 604-342-6941
Home page: www.panoramaresort.com

Snowboarding
The half-pipe is large and located off the top of the Horizon chair..... close to the First Aid station! There are some good spots in the trees, particularly towards the top, though the hard-packed base calls for a more racing-style board.

Cross country
A great variety of Nordic tracks weave out from the village and up into the valley. Stretching east and west from the base, there are over 22km of trails. If you're skiing close to the Silver Platter and encounter alpine skiers looking tired, turn them round as they probably took the wrong turn off Trappers Ridge.

Lessons and rentals
Panorama has a large and developed ski school. Lessons and improvement packages are available for all levels of skiing; many lessons last three or more hours. Children's programs cost $39 a day and six-hour improvement lessons are only $80. Inclusive First-Run Snowboard programs last three hours and cost $79.

Rental packages start from $20 (junior, $13) for skis and $35 for boards per day (half day, $25).

Lift tickets
	Adult	Teen/Senior	Junior (7-12)	Child (6 and under)
One Day	$42.06	$33.65	$21.50	$8.41
Two days	$76.64	$58.88	$37.88	$14.01

Other multi-day passes are also available at a further discount and packages offer good proportionate savings.

Getting there and around
Panorama is 18 kilometres west of the town of Invermere in the Columbia Valley, just follow the signs. It is 1½ hours north of Cranbrook and three hours from Calgary. It is also only 30 minutes from Radium Hot Springs! Transportation from Calgary can be arranged (call the Information and Reservation number); bus charters are common during the holiday periods and weekends.

Accommodation
Panorama has a small, organised village with several series of condos. All accommodation can be booked through the Reservations office (☎ 1-800-663-2929). A weekend of good skiing will cost upwards of $200 per person based on four people sharing. The condos are good, although there is a fair amount of difference between the older and newer units. It's worth asking about discounts but during the high season the resort is often full.

Après ski
Halfway up the hill there is a hut where you can get coffee and hot dogs and relax. At the bottom the new lodge and cafeteria has good food and often opens an outdoor BBQ. There are a couple of restaurants and the *Glacier Bar* has dancing. The condo units have access to a general store and are all equipped with kitchens. Some have BBQs but the standards are inconsistent. The real nightlife takes place in the many indoor and outdoor hot tubs as well as the communal BBQs.

Other
For experienced skiers with extra cash, Panorama has a large heli-skiing organization. While prices are almost 10 times the cost of your lift ticket, this is some of the world's best skiing; a day's heli-skiing here is much cheaper than an inclusive heli-package.

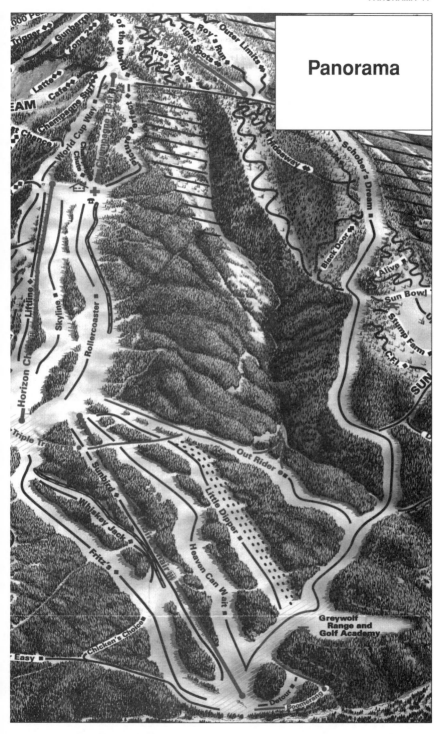

Panorama

❏ **FAIRMONT HOT SPRINGS RESORT**
Information and reservations: ☎ 250-345-6311 or ☎ 1-800-663-4979
Home page: www.fairmontresort.com

FAIRMONT HOT SPRINGS RESORT

Fairmont Hot Springs can have some good skiing although the hill remains small. The real fun of this resort is the hot springs which revive even the most weary. The hot pools may have lost some of their original charm as they are now large and developed, but they are still a great place to relax. Entrance to the pools costs $6.

Fairmont Resort is a good spot from which to visit other larger hills in the Columbia Valley – lift tickets for Kimberley, Panorama and Fernie can be arranged here. This is also an excellent place for families and you can find enough entertainment on the hill while the kids have their lessons.

The ski area has 13 runs and fortunately has good snowmaking to compensate for the fairly low snowfalls. If the snow does stay later in the season, Fairmont is a great place for skiing – as well as cycling or walking – since the lower valley can be surprisingly warm.

Accommodation

Inclusive luxury packages start from $109 per person with lift tickets. For reservations phone ☎ 1-800-663-4979.

Getting there and around

Fairmont Hot Springs is 32 kilometres south of Invermere; Panorama is 18km west of Invermere. It is 140km from Banff via a beautiful drive, 300km from Calgary and 112km north of Cranbrook, BC. As you drive either up or down the Rocky Mountain Trench along the #2 it is simply impossible to miss the sign for Fairmont Hot Springs. From the hotel area it's another three kilometres up hill to the ski field. The hotel operates a shuttle and the resort even has a small airport, although the chances are you will arrive in Fairmont by car.

KIMBERLEY

Kimberley is proof that German immigration to western Canada and its distinctly Bavarian look is both good for marketing and enjoyed by its many visitors. Like many of the southern BC ski areas, Kimberley has been in the process of being discovered

❏ **KIMBERLEY**
Base elevation: 1,280m (4,200ft)
Summit: 1,982m (6,500ft)
Vertical: 702m (2,300ft)
Lifts: 2 triples, 1 double, 3 surface (1 T-Bar, 2 handle tows)
47 Runs: 20% beginner, 60% intermediate, 20% advanced
Average snowfall: 3.35m (11ft)
Lift operating hours: 9am-4pm, night skiing Tuesday to Saturday 5-9.30pm

Contacts
Information and reservations: ☎ 250-427-4881
Kimberley Tourist Information Centre: ☎ 250-427-4838
Kimberley Vacations: ☎ 1-800-667-0871
Home page: www.kimberleyskiresort.bc.ca

for several years now and like Panorama further up the Columbia valley there is an ever-growing collection of condos and hotels at the base of the hill.

Despite the tourist facade, Kimberley remains a mining/forestry town which is friendly and relaxed. The undeveloped and entertaining ski hill is just another reason to visit this corner of BC.

Kimberley has a good variety of runs and generally good snow although, as is true with most of the region, the warm spring temperatures make the snow crusty later in the season. If the snow doesn't meet your expectations, return your pass within an hour of purchase; you'll receive a snow cheque which is valid for another day's skiing. Should you reach Kimberley after a good dumping, head for the trees off the double chair or over the back. Beginners have to choose their route fairly carefully, although the entire ridge provides a long and easy trail for practising turns. Be aware of advanced skiers appearing out of the trees!

Intermediates can have a good time trying more narrow runs and challenging their knees on a few bumps. The Easter triple chair has lots of challenging advanced terrain but the few double blacks off the main chair are really for experts only.

The lifts at Kimberley are a little slower than modern quads, but the area has been able to maintain a friendly, community feel.

Ask the locals about finding some of the less developed hot pools in the area.

Snowboarding
Boards have caught on through the valley and Kimberley is good fun when there is dry powder. The long ski-out from the triple chair can be a bit tedious on a board.

Cross country
Cross and back-country skiing are popular throughout the area. Kimberley itself has 26km of cross-country tracks at the Nordic Centre next to the Kirkwood Inn.

Lessons and rentals
Lessons are $24 per hour ($19 for 12 years and under) and private lessons start from $40 ($35 for 12 and under). Discover Skiing and snowboarding packages (lesson, handle tow lift ticket and rental) are available from $40 per day.

Ski rental is from $35 for an adult ($25 for 12 and under); snowboard rental is $40 for an adult ($30 for 12 and under).

Lift tickets

	Adult	Student (with ID)	Junior (13-18) /Senior (60+)	Child (9-12)
Full day	$35	$30	$27	$15

Children aged 8 and under ski free. Two, three, four and five-day packages (which include night skiing) are also available.

Getting there and around
The town of Kimberley is at the southern end of the Columbia Valley on highway #95a; it's only 30km from Cranbrook, the largest city in the region. Calgary is $4\frac{1}{2}$ hours away and Spokane is $3\frac{1}{2}$ hours south. If you don't have the time to enjoy the beautiful drive, Cranbrook's airport is close by with several daily flights from both Vancouver and Calgary. Once in Kimberley just follow the signs up hill to the base of the ski area.

Accommodation and après ski
Kimberley has been developing into a fairly significant resort over the last few years, and the seven on-site properties can accommodate 1,200 people. There are many other

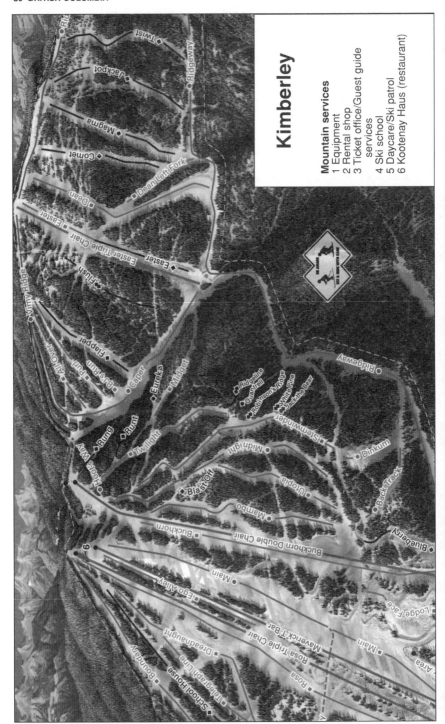

Kimberley

Mountain services
1 Equipment
2 Rental shop
3 Ticket office/Guest guide services
4 Ski school
5 Daycare/Ski patrol
6 Kootenay Haus (restaurant)

hotels down in town and in Cranbrook; for details call **Kimberley Tourist Information Office** (☎ 250-427-4838). Inclusive ski vacations at B&Bs, hotels, motels, chalets and condos can be booked through **Kimberley Vacations** (☎ 1-800-667-0871).

On-hill rooms/condos start from $65 and even upscale rooms remain fairly reasonable; try *Mountain Edge Resort Inn* (☎ 250-427-5381 or ☎ 1-800-525-6622) or *Inn West/Kirkwood Inn* (☎ 250-427-7616 or ☎ 1-800-663-4755).

If you don't feel like cooking in your condo drive down to town and stroll through the **Platzl**. Obviously the best food is German and rumour has it that the imported beer was fortified in the Alps. If German food is not your favourite, this old mining town still has good old Canadian food at reasonable prices.

FERNIE SNOW VALLEY

Just on the western side of the Great Divide, nestled in the south-east corner of British Colombia, Fernie offers great skiing and buckets of snow. The weather is somewhat milder than in other areas and the town is relaxed and friendly. Legend has it that a child was born in a bear's den; the bear was hungry from his winter sleep, and in short a battle ensued, from which the young mountain man triumphed. 'Griz' now brings the huge snow quantities to this old mining town and in turn the town holds a festival in his honour each year.

The ski area is essentially one large face with the large Cedar Bowl off the eastern side. Once the expansions are complete the area should be at least 50% larger. For the moment, the lower half of the mountain is almost all blue and green, so beginners and average intermediates can have a good time off the El-quad and the Deer triple chairs. Overall Fernie is quite steep so green fans can give themselves a bit of a challenge.

The Cedar Bowl caters for intermediates to experts and is a source of great pleasure in heavy snowfall years. The Boomerang triple and the far side of the Lizard Bowl have some great black tree-runs with all the bumps and snow one could ask for. Intermediates get the rest of the hill. You'll enjoy the upper areas, but will find yourselves skiing green near the bottom – a good chance to get the feel for softer snow. Fernie is a great all round mountain with an ever-growing number of loyal fans.

Fernie also has a large system of Snow-Cat skiing; $195 a day, $135 for half a day – this is nothing compared to the usual charge of $300 a day.

Cross country
There are 15km of track-set and groomed trails from the resort's base.

Snowboarding
The fantastic powder makes Fernie a great boarding destination.

Lessons and rentals
Discover Skiing inclusive packages are $39 per day and $49 for the boarding version. You can also improve your powder skiing for around $40 (two hours' rental and a lesson are included) and regular half-day lessons on boards or skis are $25 – good value!

Basic rentals for an adult are $19 (child, $14) or $28 for good quality skis; $25 for boards.

Lift tickets

	Adult	Youth/student (13-25 with ID)/ Senior (65+)	Child (6-12)
Full day	$36	$29	$15
Half day	$29	$25	$15

With these prices it's hardly worth getting a half-day ticket. Three or more days are

Fernie – Alpine Resort

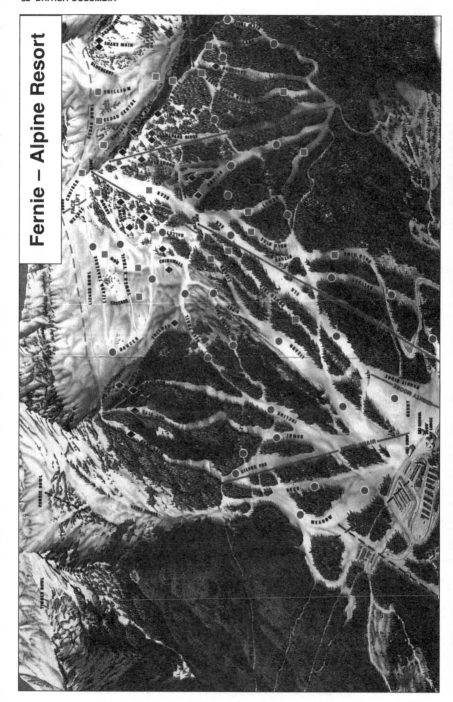

$32/day for adults, $25 for youth/student/senior and $15 for a child, except over Christmas/New Year.

Getting there and around

Fortunately the Snow Valley is reasonably accessible from southern Alberta and BC. Just inside BC along route #3 Fernie is an easy hour from Cranbrook and three hours from Calgary. When approaching the town just look up to find the slopes. Transport can be arranged from Cranbrook and Calgary airports and a shuttle runs from the town for $4 return.

Accommodation and après ski

Staying up at the mountain doesn't have to be too expensive, especially if a few people get together and rent a condo. The main hotel is *Griz Inn* with rooms ranging from $85-$350. Packages are much better value; lodging, lifts, meal plan, improvement sessions and après ski activities for a family cost $170 for two days and $477 for five days between Sunday and Thursday. *Wolf's Den Mountain Lodge* is more affordable with rooms from $76-$115, but it does not have a pool. There are eight other relatively affordable hotels in Fernie itself and a youth hostel. A good B&B costs from $35 per night. Everything can be booked through the main Reservations office (☎ 1-888-754-7325 or ☎ 250-423-9284).

Unless you plan on going at Christmas/New Year, arriving in town without booking accommodation shouldn't be a problem – just go along to the friendly reservations office.

The *Day Lodge* has a cafeteria and a bar, *Barry's Bar,* with après ski music. Lunch can be bought mid-mountain. There is also an Italian restaurant and *Griz Inn* has a restaurant and lounge.

Other

If you drive north from Fernie you'll travel through the beautiful valley adjoining the towns of Sparwood and Elkford, both of which have small, snowy ski areas with friendly people and night skiing. The valley that route #43 runs through is also very popular with snowmobilers, and unfortunately, avalanches.

❑ FERNIE SNOW VALLEY
Base elevation: 1,067m (3,500ft)
Summit: 1,798m (5,900ft)
Vertical: 731m (2,400ft)
Lifts: 1 quad, 2 triples, 4 surface – watch out for two more quads
58+Runs: 30% beginner, 40% intermediate, 30% advanced
Average snowfall: 875cm (29ft) and often more.
Lift operating hours: 9am-4pm

Contacts
Information: ☎ 250-423-4655
Reservations: ☎ 1-888-754-7325 or ☎ 250-423-9284
24hr snow phone: ☎ 250-423-3555, Calgary ☎ 403-244-6665
Ski school information and bookings: ☎ 250-423-3515
Home page: www.elkvalley.net/far

Central & northern British Columbia

Given the enormous size of Canada and all its provinces it is a relative travesty to write off an area larger than England as one simple region. But this giant hinterland is only accessible on certain routes and over 80% of Canadians live fairly close to the American border. Sadly the northern part of BC is an area generally unknown to many Canadians. While much of northern Canada is being explored by mining and drilling companies, British Columbia's northern territory is particularly rich in minerals and lumber and for a long time developers have been motivated to open it to settlement; however their plans have been opposed by environmental groups.

For over 100 years now, non-native Indians have been travelling north – many in search of gold in BC's Caribou country and even further north in the Klondike. The north-west coast of BC is slowly being discovered by tourists for its dramatic beauty and unique wildlife. The towns and cities of the central province are vibrant communities with their economies tied strongly to British Columbia's resource economy.

Although much of central BC is a tourist destination throughout the summer months, the northern communities become particularly quiet and isolated during winter.

Prince George, one of BC's five largest cities, is located in central BC and is the principal junction for people travelling west from central Alberta and those coming north from southern BC. With almost 70,000 people this resource-based city has had enough wealth to spur the development of winter activities. Further east, **Smithers** is an important administrative town with a vibrant community of 5,000 and a good mountain. Further west towards Prince Rupert and the coast, **Terrace,** with 10,000 people, is gaining some acclaim in the skiing world with its interesting runs and excellent snowfalls.

People heading for the Yukon in winter will discover a certain lack of light, but can encounter some skiing along the way – lift lines simply don't exist up here.

Getting around the north

Road maintenance is very good in BC and larger cities such as Prince George are easy to visit any time of the year. If you're planning to visit the Yukon over winter, the reception will be warm, but the trip long and cold. As so many of the mountain passes are all but impassable, most routes going north from Prince George veer east to the flatter land, meeting up with the Alaska Highway as it enters BC at Dawson Creek.

The principal route running east-west through central BC is highway #16. To go further north from Prince George the #97 is the best route and the #37 further west is about half paved. After Vancouver and Whistler, traditionalists can continue north on route #99 eventually meeting up with #97 west of Kamloops, from there it is clear sailing to Prince George and the Yukon – a couple of days later!

Serious driving precautions must be taken in the north. Not so much because of the roads, but because gas stations can be few and far between and engine trouble can leave you stranded for long periods during winter.

Skiing the North

Although the many ski areas north of the Okanagan and west of Jasper are quite small and undeveloped, several have over 500 vertical metres (1,600ft) and at least two have snow accumulations well over 10 metres (32ft)!

Resorts are never crowded and are often partially run by local volunteers. The ski season generally ends in March – not because of poor conditions but because people have skied so much that they're moving on to spring activities. While the temperature gets progressively colder the further north you go, the concept of a lift line is simply unknown.

Barely far enough north to even constitute central BC, *The Hills Health Ranch* (☎ 250-791-5225) is a relax-and-be-healthy type of place with over 200km of cross country and all the instruction and equipment you could ask for. Weekend packages start from $259 per person. Located near 100 Mile House on #97, The Hills is a moderate day's drive from Vancouver.

There is also a little skiing near Williams Lake on **Mount Timothy** (☎ 250-395-3772). Mount Timothy has a fairly low snowfall, but there are 25 runs and a 260-metre vertical. Clinton also has a small hill as does Cottonwood, west of Quesnel.

Hart Highlands (☎ 250-962-8006) is a tiny community-run hill within the city limits of Prince George. Twenty five kilometres from the city is **Tabor Mountain** (☎ 250-963-7889) with two lifts, 10 runs and almost 250m of vertical. **Purden Lake,** east of Prince George, and **Fort St James** to the west both have small hills.

It is always a good idea to call ahead before skiing anywhere in the north as resorts don't necessarily remain open every day. Often the snow is saved for the weekends and holidays.

POWDER KING SKI VILLAGE

Powder King, 200 kilometres north of Prince George and an easy 70 kilometres east of MacKenzie, is one of those great mountains that is just too damn far away. This mountain should be a destination for all powder worshippers with annual snowfalls topping 12 metres (38ft). It also has over 600 metres vertical (1,900ft) and great, friendly uncrowded skiing and boarding. A great way to warm up to a heli-skiing adventure.

Powder King has one triple chair and two surface lifts and most facilities. Skiing starts in November and continues till the spring and there is some accommodation available at the base. For information and reservations phone ☎ 250-997-6323.

Closer to Mackenzie, **Little Mac** (☎ 604-997-5283) also has some skiing.

North again on the other side of the Great Divide you can find some skiing around Dawson Creek, Chetwynd and, way up in Fort Nelson, there are a few runs at **Northpoint** (☎ 604-774-4258).

SKI SMITHERS

Just above the town of Smithers, almost 400km west of Prince George, this resort is the largest in the north. Smithers is a good intermediate mountain with consistent snow. There are 18 runs and if you can find a local to guide you it is possible to ski all the way to Smithers town, but don't try on your own – the north is a tough place to be lost.

One chair and three surface lifts serve 18 trails and 530m (1700ft) vertical. Smithers also has cross-country skiing and there is plenty of accommodation and a fair selection of restaurants and pubs.

For information and reservations phone ☎ 250-847-5327

SHAMES MOUNTAIN

At the narrowing of the Skeena River, just 140 kilometres from Prince Rupert and the coast, Shames Mountain is the grand culmination of any quest for powder. This mountain has 18 runs (the majority are intermediate) and three lifts. The double chair accesses essentially all the runs on this 500m (1,600ft) vertical. There are a few good, long advanced runs and all the skiing is on cut trails. The real draw to Shames (and

Terrace) is the snow. **Annual accumulations are close to 14 metres (40ft)!** The only threat to constant, good skiing is avalanches, so always stay in bounds. The proximity to the coast does mean the snow is rather heavy but good fitness will permit great skiing.

Accommodation can be found in Terrace (40km away). For information and reservations phone ☎ 250-635-3773.

Other slopes can be found in Prince Rupert, Kitimat and Stewart on the American border.

YUKON

If you are lucky enough to visit Canada's north during winter, the skiing is a bit on the cold side, but, hey, you'll be north of 60. Watson Lake and Dawson both have ski clubs, and Whitehorse locals ski at the very friendly, community-run **Sima Ski Area** (☎ 403-667-7547).

PART 3: ALBERTA

Skiing Alberta

Sharing the Great Divide as its border with BC, the province of Alberta descends toward the east from the Rocky Mountains, through the foothills and down to the Great Plains. Western Canada's Prairies then continue through two more provinces before meeting up with Ontario and the Canadian Shield.

Over two thirds of Alberta's $2\frac{1}{2}$ million inhabitants live in the province's two principal cities, Edmonton and Calgary, and thousands of these city folk were raised on skis in the nearby mountain parks of Banff, Jasper and Kananaskis Country. Calgary, which has long been known for its summertime rodeo, the Stampede, gained world acclaim in 1988 when it hosted a very successful Winter Olympics.

The central western provinces of Canada are renowned for their cold winter weather and the truly wicked wind chills that can blow across the open land and drop the temperature to unbearable levels. However, in the mountains of Alberta there is some shelter from the prairie weather and southern Alberta itself has a unique wind called the *Chinook* which can warm the greater Calgary area to well above freezing, even during the depths of winter.

Most of Alberta is relatively flat, with the land being moulded by rivers and ancient oceanic sediment. The most recognisable photographs of the Canadian Rockies show the mountainous region of Alberta. While the parks of Jasper and Banff have gained international acclaim, the beautiful Kananaskis is still very much the domain of locals. Further south, the Crowsnest Pass region is the most southerly Canadian route through the Rockies leading to the towns of southern BC.

Obviously the vast majority of downhill skiing is found in the Rockies, though there are other, smaller and sometimes more convenient hills throughout the Prairies. For fans of cross country and snowmobiling, there are plenty of great adventures to be had. Within two hours of Calgary are some of Canada's oldest and best-known ski resorts, including Lake Louise and Banff, as well as the much undervalued Kananaskis Provincial Park, home to the Olympic ski hill, Nakiska.

Although the Alberta mountains are one of Canada's premier ski areas there are those who continue to stay away for fear of the cold. Fair enough. But while Alberta does have periods of extreme cold these do not last long and the old adage of 'it's a dry cold' does indeed apply. A good jacket and face protection is often enough. In fact, newcomers to Alberta worry more about dry skin than staying warm!

As a result of the cold dry air, the snow in Alberta is lighter than in BC. Accumulations are generally somewhat lower than coastal areas, though Sunshine Village boasts over nine metres annually.

If you're travelling through the region on work or in pursuit of great cross-country or snowmobiling, it's worth throwing your skis in the truck as one of Alberta's 32 regional areas can never be far away. The capital city of Edmonton has three small slopes right in town and the central northern region has over six areas that can offer a ski-fix.

Getting around Alberta

If you've driving to Alberta from the east or west it is likely that you've travelled at least some of your journey along the Trans-Canada Highway which makes its way

❏ **ALBERTA – TOURIST INFORMATION**

Calgary Convention and Visitor Bureau*
Calgary Tower
Mall Level
9th Ave
SW Calgary
(☎ 403-263-8510)

Travel Alberta
PO Box 2500
Edmonton
Alberta T5J 2Z4
☎ 1-800-661-8888 or
☎ 403-427-4321
or ☎ 403-678-5277

*Also at Calgary International Airport on both the arrival and departure floors.

through southern Alberta and Calgary. Calgary and Edmonton are joined by a good dual-lane highway that also links them with the mountain parks to the west. Both Calgary and Edmonton have international airports. By car, Calgary is one hour from Banff and Kananaskis Parks, and Edmonton is four hours from Jasper.

If you choose Alberta as a ski, or simply a winter, destination it is imperative that you are prepared for difficult road conditions and temperatures which often fall below -30°C. The Canadian Prairies are notorious for low temperatures, and the roads can often be hidden under blowing snow. However, these are not good enough reasons for rejecting the idea of a ski vacation here.

Most people who fly to Alberta will arrive in Calgary; fortunately the section of the Trans-Canada between Calgary and Banff is well patrolled and maintained. Once in the Bow Valley around Banff distances are not extreme and the roads are generally well gravelled. Gas prices here are the lowest in Canada. Bus services are available all over the province and are frequent between Calgary and Banff. Companies such as Brewster and Laidlaw operate services regularly from the airport to the mountain towns. One-way tickets cost around $20 and can be purchased at the arrivals area.

❏ **REGIONAL SKI AREAS**
Please note that the area code (403) may change in 1999.
Drayton Valley & Brazeau Ski Area ☎ 403-542-2837
Drumheller Valley Ski Club ☎ 403-823-2277
Fairview Ski Club ☎ 403-835-4725
Grizzly Ridge (Slave Lake) ☎ 403-849-2490
Gwynne Valley Ski Area (Wetaskiwin) ☎ 403-352-3515
Hidden Valley Ski Area (Elkwater) ☎ 403-893-3961
Innisfail Ski Club ☎ 403-227-5155
Kinosoo Ridge (Grand Centre) ☎ 403-826-3171
Little Smoky Ski Area (Fahler) ☎ 403-837-8144
Long Lake Ski Hill (Thorhild) ☎ 403-576-2161
Manning & District ☎ 403-836-3820
Medicine Lodge (Ponoka) ☎ 403-748-2025
Misery Mountain (Peace River) ☎ 403-624-4881
Mistahiya Ski Area (Czar) ☎ 403-842-3354
Misty Ridge Ski Club (Barrhead) ☎ 403-674-4242
Mount Joy Ski Hill (Lloydminster) ☎ 403-745-2547
Nitehawk (Grand Prairie) ☎ 403-532-6637
Pass Powder Keg (Coleman) ☎ 403-562-8334
Silver Summit (Edson) ☎ 403-447-4476
Spring Lake Winter Resort (Hythe) ☎ 403-356-3045
Tawatinaw Valley (Westlock) ☎ 403-698-2212
Valley Ski Club (Castor) ☎ 403-879-2106
Vista Ridge All Season Park (Fort McMurray) ☎ 403-743-8651
Whispering Pines (Worsley) ☎ 403-685-3965

Edmonton

Alberta's capital, Edmonton, does not enjoy the same proximity to the mountains as Calgary but it does host slightly longer, snowier winters and certainly has an equally dedicated group of skiers. Drive through central Edmonton anytime during winter and you will undoubtedly see people skiing on the many little hills that surround the central river valley. If you would like to see Edmontonians really performing, drive out to Jasper and enjoy the uncrowded slopes of Marmot Basin.

Ski Clubs
Edmonton Ski Club ☎ 403-465-0852
Rabbit Hill (Edmonton) ☎ 403-955-2440
Snow Valley Ski Club (Edmonton) ☎ 403-434-3991
Sunridge Ski Area (Edmonton) ☎ 403-449-6555

Good cross-country areas can be found throughout the city and province, however it is worth driving east to Strathcona for extensive opportunities.

Canyon Ski Area (☎ 403-346-5580) in Red Deer is the largest non-mountain ski area in Alberta with 11 runs and 164m vertical. Canyon has five lifts (the double chair is open at weekends only) and a fun luge track. Red Deer is halfway between Edmonton and Calgary.

Calgary

With fair claim to the title 'Gateway to the Rockies', Calgary is a wealthy and growing oil city with a cosmopolitan and active population. While the Stampede has been Calgary's traditional draw, the city's proximity to Banff and its great facilities have made it one of Canada's major winter destinations.

Although most cities in Canada have the right to claim a strong winter sporting tradition, Calgary took first honours when the city hosted a very successful Winter Olympics in 1988. While the games were extremely popular, particularly with the thousands of locals who volunteered, the lasting legacy has been the infrastructure. Partially due to the huge television receipts earned by the games, the Calgary Olympics Committee has been able to keep all the venues open and profitable. The games were so successful that Calgary is bidding to host the games in 2010.

Accommodation
Calgary is a city of nearly 800,000 people and it has hundreds of hotel options for any budget. You will almost always find a room during winter and often at reduced prices compared to the summer.

For further information contact **Calgary Convention and Visitor Bureau** (☎ 403-263-8510) or **Travel Alberta** (☎ 403-678-5277 or ☎ 403-427-4321 or ☎ 1-800-661-8888).

CANADA OLYMPIC PARK

Canada Olympic Park (COP) is a tiny ski area with a significant sporting history found within Calgary's city limits. The hill, originally named Paskapoo, on which it is built was bought by the government when Calgary was awarded the 1988 Winter Olympics. Through the 1980s the area was transformed into a world-class site for luge, bobsleigh and ski-jumping. If you have trouble finding it, just look to the western side of Calgary for the 70- and 90-metre ski-jumps standing atop the hill. The top of the giant 90-metre jump is also a popular place for weddings and receptions – there's only one way to go!

COP is a great place to learn to ski or snowboard and the snowmaking ensures a full season. If you're interested in trying bobsleighing you can join the club or dish out $100 for the run of a lifetime. As for the ski jumps, you need to start as a child, or train with Eddy the Eagle on the British National Team!

For information and reservations phone ☎ 403-247-5452

Cross country

There are plenty of opportunities right in Calgary city. Providing the unpredictable snowfall is generous most parks are fine for an easy ski, and Shaganappi golf course, south west of downtown, is a popular spot with a few bumps.

WINTERGREEN

The other ski area which could claim to be Calgary's is four kilometres from the hamlet of **Bragg Creek**, 30 minutes west of the city. Wintergreen is a relaxed and friendly hill which is step two in a three step plan for Calgarians to ski the big mountains; the first step is Canada Olympic Park and the third the Rockies. With very affordable lift tickets and a great deal more terrain than Canada Olympic Park, Wintergreen is ideal for young families and new skiers and boarders. Lifts operate from 10am to 4pm. The night skiing (Tuesday to Saturday, 4-9pm) and tubing (4-9pm, Fridays, 10am-4pm weekends and holidays) are close enough to Calgary for you to take a few runs after work. The snowboard park is well lit through the evening.

The ski area has ten distinct runs (three beginner, four intermediate, and three advanced) and five lifts with the potential for future development. The golf course at the base of the hill provides five kilometres of cross country trails.

Getting there and around

Bragg Creek is directly west of Calgary along highway #22; Bragg Creek can also be reached from the Trans-Canada, heading west from Calgary. Southland Transportation (☎ 403-287-1335) charges $5 for a round trip ticket from Calgary; pick up is possible from several shopping centres in Calgary.

If you are including Wintergreen in a ski trip through the Rockies, you will not be able to reach the resorts of the Kananaskis via Bragg Creek as the connecting road is closed during winter. Returning to the #1 is just as fast anyway.

❑ WINTERGREEN
Information: ☎ 403-949-5100
Snow phone: ☎ 403-244-6665
Southland Bus Transportation: ☎ 403-287-1335

Wintergreen

TRAILS

● 2 Spruce Grouse
● 3 Whitetail
● 4 Mule Deer

■ 1 Sparrow Hawk
■ 5 Raven
■ 7 Hoot Owl
■ 8 Lynx

◆ 6 Falcon
◆ 9 Bobcat
◆ 10 Cougar

FUTURE SKI TERRAIN

QUAD

MOOSE MEADOW
T-BAR

SNOWBOARD
PARK

EAGLE'S NEST
DOUBLE CHAIR

DEER RUN

LODGE

PATROL

Banff

Banff is one of Canada's premier resorts and it's an ideal base from which to ski the Rockies. As both a summer and winter destination, it is the heart of the Alberta Rockies and Banff's 7,000 or so permanent residents play host to tens of thousands of visitors each year from around the world.

Along with the beautiful mountain views and relatively good weather, people are attracted to the relaxed yet sophisticated feel of the town. Part of Banff's appeal is its wonderful variety of outdoor activities, all within 1½ hours of a major city and international airport.

Location
Nestled on the western edge of Alberta, the name 'Banff' refers to both the town and the National Park in which it lies. The park gates are a one hour drive west from Calgary along the Trans-Canada; the town is fifteen minutes further on. From Vancouver, Banff is a nine-hour drive east – providing the roads are clear.

Skiing
Banff National Park is in many ways the home of skiing in western Canada. The park's principal ski fields can be reached within an hour from Banff town: Norquay and Mystic Ridge (10 minutes), Sunshine Village and Goat's Eye Mountain (20 minutes) and Lake Louise (one hour). Lake Louise is a resort area independent of Banff which offers first class accommodation and a village atmosphere.

In conjunction with the excellent downhill skiing, heli-skiing can be booked in central Banff and excellent cross-country skiing can be found everywhere. Perhaps the greatest spot for cross-country fans and biathlon athletes is the **Canmore Nordic Centre**, situated in the town of Canmore, twenty minutes east of Banff. To obtain maps of the surrounding area and for cross-country ideas visit **Banff Park Visitor Information Centre** (☎ 403-762-1550) centrally located on Banff Avenue.

Getting there and around
Banff is 130 kilometres from Calgary. If you don't have a car, you can take a Greyhound or Brewster bus from the Greyhound garage in downtown Calgary for around $25 one way. Or you could join the hitch-hikers along the Trans-Canada. Coming from the east, Greyhound has regular services throughout BC. Several of the ski resorts have Snow Shuttles for day skiers from Calgary.

Once in Banff, you can walk almost everywhere. For longer trips, or on cold nights, take a cab or catch the Banff Transportation Trolley that runs regularly throughout town ($1.50). Shuttles operate between the hotels and the ski fields.

Accommodation
With over 10,000 beds in the Banff area, the choice is staggering. So are the prices. Because Banff is both a National and a World Heritage Park there are strict restrictions on expansion and the government has stated that the building boom of the 1980s will be the last. This has had an obvious effect upon the supply-demand ratio. The restrictions in the Park have caused significant growth in the old mining town of Canmore, situated just east of the Park gates.

It shouldn't be too difficult to find a room during the winter months, but reservations are essential during the Christmas/New Year season and prices tend to be higher. Easter is also popular and locals flock out to the mountains on long weekends. For further information on accommodation stop in at the Travel Alberta office (☎ 403-678-5277 or ☎ 1-800-661-8888) just off the Trans-Canada in Canmore or call **Banff/Lake Louise Central Reservations** (☎ 1-800-661-1676 or ☎ 403-760-5200 or 403-762-5561).

Both Banff and Canmore are filled with mid-range hotels that are geared towards skiers during the winter months but only a few can be listed here. Most hotels offer reasonable value for a ski resort.

In Banff the most central is the old, but recently renovated, ***Mount Royal Hotel*** (☎ 403-762-3331 or ☎ 1-800-267-3035). Rooms tend to be small but well appointed. Winter prices range from $84 to $250+ for a de-luxe suite. Also central is ***Banff Park Lodge*** (☎ 403-762-4433 or ☎ 1-800-661-9266) with rooms from around $110.

A little way out of town are the ***Tunnel Mountain Chalets*** (☎ 403-762-4515 or ☎ 1-800-661-1859) with units suitable for groups available from $150. If you enjoy skiing Mount Norquay you can ski-out to ***Timberline Lodge*** (☎ 403-762-2281) from $130.

The most famous and luxurious hotel in Banff is the Canadian Pacific ***Banff Springs Hotel*** (☎ 403-762-2211 or Canadian Pacific Hotels Reservations ☎ 1-800-441-1414). And it is as beautiful as the photos. You're doing well if you find a room in low season for around $160, however you can easily spend hundreds more.

Budget

There are really only two budget options in Banff, if you don't count winter camping. Reservations are essential in both. Just across the river at the top of town is the ***YWCA*** (☎ 403-762-3560 or ☎ 1-800-813-4138) with dorm beds for around $20. ***Hostelling International (Banff)*** (☎ 403-762-4122) has a more attractive, less central youth hostel on Tunnel Mountain Drive with dorm beds for under $20.

The **Southern Alberta Hostelling Association** (☎ 403-762-4122) maintains an excellent system of hostels throughout the Rockies. Several stay open all winter and make for great cross-country bases. The Banff hostel is connected with an international booking system so beds can be reserved from hostels around the world.

Après ski

As the principal source of income for Banff is tourism you may feel short on funds but you won't on culinary choices. All the hotels have restaurants, and pancakes with maple syrup are always available in the morning! You shouldn't have to pay more than $25 for a very good meal. International cuisine is also easy to find but a touch more expensive.

Bumper's Beef House situated at the far end of town, is a bit of a walk, but the Alberta beef makes the trip worthwhile. The menu does have other choices. ***The Keg***, another steak restaurant, has branches throughout western Canada – it's so popular there are two in Banff. ***Melissa's Missteak*** is relaxed and affordable any time of day; excellent breakfasts are served here. ***Paris's Restaurant*** in the centre of town is not a French restaurant, but was named after an early Banff family. The food is great, particularly the fresh lobster. ***The Rose and Crown*** is an English-style restaurant/pub that remains popular with the locals. ***Wild Bill's*** is for those who like a country atmosphere and a little line dancing.

Banff also has a ***Hard Rock Café*** and a generous selection of coffee shops and a good bagel place. Banff Springs Hotel has a deli, pub and a first-class dining room. ***Rimrock Hotel*** near the base of Sulphur Mountain also has a very upscale restaurant with great views of the valley. Needless to say Banff has a ***McDonald's***. Canmore houses the rest of the fast-food joints. There is also a Safeway in the centre of town, as well as plenty of places to find beer and provisions. However, it is worth venturing out to visit the many excellent restaurants and pubs.

The greatest pleasure after a hard day skiing is a visit to the **Upper Hot Springs**. A favourite for over 100 years, the springs help revive even the most weary bodies. They are also a great way to recover after spending the whole day in freezing temperatures. To get to the pools just cross the river at the top of Banff Avenue and follow the signs.

MOUNT NORQUAY

This is the closest ski area to Banff town and the views of the runs from town are only bettered by the views of Banff and the surrounding valley from the mountain. Traditionally Mount Norquay was home to the true experts and the true beginners, but with the expansion to Mystic Ridge the area has opened up to intermediates.

Norquay also has a wonderful new base lodge – hopefully it will last longer than the first which burnt down shortly after construction.

Mystic Ridge and Norquay is certainly the smallest ski area of the valley, but it is still worth a visit. For genuine expert skiers the best argument for making the trip is called Lone Pine – one of the steepest slopes in North America. In fact skiers can win awards based on the number of runs they manage on the expert-only North American chair. The perennial drawback to Mystic Ridge and Norquay is the snow – often the last to take hold and the first to leave (or slide off) due to the vertical drop. Fortunately there is fairly comprehensive snow-making.

The Mystic Ridge high-speed quad has some steep, groomed blue and black runs which provide a good opportunity for beginners to challenge themselves and for speedsters to learn to fly. The runs with bumps can be enjoyable, but check the conditions first as the snow can be unpleasantly crusty.

The other attraction to this area is the night skiing; the lights are turned on every Friday and Saturday night (4-9pm) from 26 December until the end of the season – the views of Banff are fantastic. While other resorts may be busy, you'll rarely stand in line at Norquay.

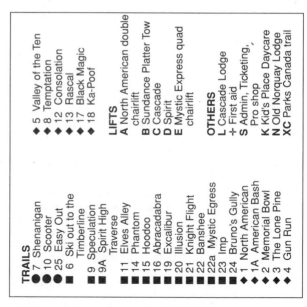

Mount Norquay

❏ **MOUNT NORQUAY**
Base elevation: 1,634m (5,350ft)
Summit: 2,133m (7,000ft)
Vertical: 503m (1,650ft)
Lifts: 2 quads, 2 doubles and 3 surface
25 runs: 5 beginner, 9 intermediate, 11 advanced
Average snowfall: low – a great deal of snowmaking
Lift operating hours: 9am-4pm

Contacts
Information and reservations: ☎ 403-762-4421
24hr snow phone: ☎ 403-760-7704
Ski school: ☎ 403-760-7716
Home page: www.banffnorquay.com

Snowboarding
Norquay is doing its best to attract boarders and now has a full snowboard park.

Cross country
Norquay has some beautiful tracks running north into the valley. Just skate past the base of the lifts and enjoy one of the most accessible valleys in the area. Routes are marked.

Lessons and rentals
Lessons with rentals start from $35 per hour; private lessons go for a steep $55. There are a great variety of junior packages starting from around $30 for equipment, ticket and lesson. Norquay has one of Canada's premier racing schools.

Lift tickets

	Adult	Senior (65+)/Youth (13-18)	Junior (6-12)
Full Day	$35	$29	$15
Morning	$29	$24	$15
Afternoon	$27	$22	$15
Night	$19	$18	$10

Getting there and around
Norquay is literally straight up hill from Banff and can be seen from town. A shuttle runs from some of the hotels.

SUNSHINE VILLAGE
Sunshine is the oldest operating ski field in the Alberta Rockies and definitely has the best snow in the area. It is also the only resort in Banff National Park with on-site accommodation. In 1995 Goat's Eye Mountain was opened, significantly expanding the area's terrain. Sunshine remains the major destination for local snowboarders and has the longest season in Alberta – often staying open until June.

It takes 20 minutes in a six-person gondola to reach the Sunshine Village area from the parking lot. In the past, skiers used to climb that far! However, now that Goat's Eye Mountain is an up and running success you may want to hop off at the second of the three stations to catch its high-speed quad. As you ride up the gondola keep an eye on the frozen waterfalls – you may spot a climber or two! Most of Sunshine is above the tree line and if you ride up the Continental Divide chair you actually cross into BC for a short time. Even the melting snow in the summer is a bit schizophrenic, some heading west and the rest east! With the exception of Goat's Eye and the excel-

Sunshine
Village
Goat's Eye
Mountain

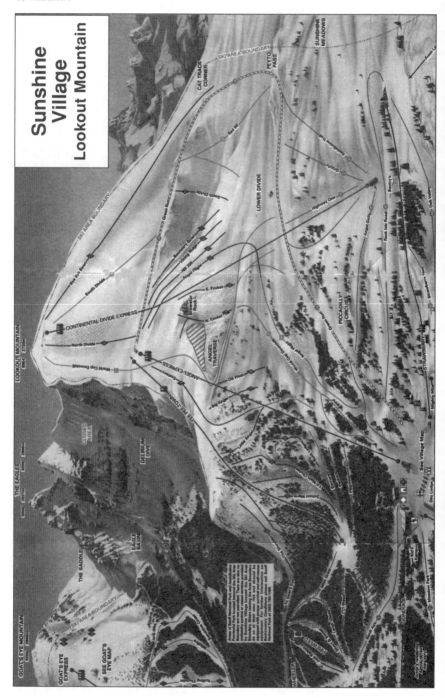

Sunshine
Village
Lookout Mountain

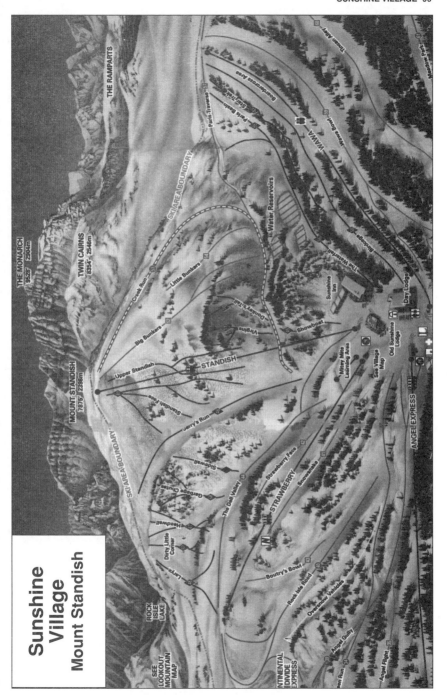

Sunshine Village
Mount Standish

lent ski-out to the parking lot, most of the runs end up at the village area which is the centre for everything; food, accommodation, rentals, etc.

The high-speed Angel quad has relieved congestion and leads to the best intermediate and advanced skiing on Lookout Mountain – this was the main hill before Goat's Eye was opened. From the top of Angel it is a nice run to the Continental Divide chair which has recently been upgraded to a high-speed quad, or down to the Tee Pee Town double with some of Sunshine's steepest and bumpiest black runs – experts only. Do be mindful of the enormous cliff off to your right as you descend.

The runs off the Standish chair and the WaWa T-bar remain popular with snowboarders and those who enjoy short, interesting runs.

Since the opening of Goat's Eye the traditional complaints of short runs and limited choice have seemed to diminish. This new area with its long blue and black runs as well as some trees should continue to bring new fans.

The snow at Sunshine is excellent and except for the odd white-out the area does live up to its name. The top of Goat's Eye is very exposed and needs fences to keep its snow. This is traditionally a hill for intermediate skiers and spring skiing is often the real attraction. Sunglasses or goggles and sunscreen are even more important here with the lack of trees. The area is large and diverse, though perhaps the published number of runs is a bit generous.

Snowboarding
This is very popular all over Sunshine because of the large amount of powder and the great jumps. Many locals take up the sport here so there are plenty of instructors and renting equipment is easy. Minor competitions are also held here.

Lessons and rentals
One of the advantages to on-site accommodation is the availability of extended lessons. Sunshine offers an inclusive Ski Week for around $400. Group lessons go for $20 per hour and private lessons for $45 per hour. Rentals are quick and easy from the top of the gondola.

Lift tickets

	Adult	Senior (65+)/Youth* (13-18)	Child (6-12)
Full day	$46	$38	$15

* Students with ID are also entitled to the Youth reduction.

The relative costs are quickly reduced if you buy one of the many package deals available. For around $100 you can buy a Sunshine card which entitles you to two free days

---

❏ SUNSHINE VILLAGE
Base elevation: 1,658m (5,440ft)
Summit: 2,730m (8,954ft)
Vertical: 1,050m (3,514ft)
Lifts: 1 gondola, 3 quads, 1 triple, 4 double and 5 surface
61 Runs: 20% beginner, 60% intermediate and 20% advanced
Average snowfall: 1040cm (33ft)

Contacts
Information and reservations: ☎ 403-762-6500 (Banff) or ☎ 403-531-0750 (Calgary)
Sunshine Village Ski Resort: (☎ 1-800-372-9583 or ☎ 403-762-6555)
Sunshine Inn ski packages: ☎ 1-800-661-1676
Snow phone: ☎ 403-760-7669
Ski school: ☎ 403-762-6560
Home page: www.skibanff.com

skiing and a reduction every other ski day; cards can be bought at the hill or in shops in Calgary or Banff.

Getting there and around
The parking area for Sunshine is just twenty minutes west of Banff and the ski area is the highest in the Canadian Rockies. Even though one of the runs crosses into BC, Sunshine is well within Alberta and Calgary is a 1¹/₂ hour drive along the Trans-Canada. None of the runs can be seen from the highway or even from the base of the gondola. Fortunately the access road is paved and in good condition. A shuttle runs between the hill, Banff and Canmore.

Accommodation and après ski
This is covered in the Banff section with the exception of the on-site option (Sunshine Inn ☎ 1-800-661-1676) at the top of the gondola. Staying on the mountain affords longer days of skiing and fresh tracks in the morning. Many different packages are available and a room with skiing starts from around $80 a single, or $115 for a double.

LAKE LOUISE
This is probably Alberta's best known ski area and has long been on the World Cup circuit. Lake Louise is the largest single ski area in Canada and one day is simply not enough. Across the valley is the lake that is renowned for its emerald colour. Sitting on the lake's edge is the majestic *Château Lake Louise*, one of Canada's top hotels. After a tough day on the slopes, you can sit back in one of its first-class dining rooms and listen for the avalanches falling off the glacier on the far side of the lake.

The ski area itself is massive and encompasses three mountain faces with a fantastic variety of slopes. The front has long, moderate slopes that are much easier to enjoy than in past years, due to a couple of high-speed quads. These offer good, consistent runs to skiers of all abilities. The summit is still accessed by a one-person platter lift as a result of the steepness, resulting in fairly large lines.

If you're new to skiing you'll want to give the summit's treeless bumps a miss. Wiwaxy is an excellent run for beginners with several kilometres of long, sweeping turns. Juniper is the intermediate version but it can be crowded. From the top of the Eagle chair a continuous intermediate run can be followed all the way to the base. Be aware of icy patches.

The backside loses its sun much earlier, but offers a great variety of bowl skiing, particularly for strong skiers. It's under the Paradise triple chair that you'll find the real

---

❏ LAKE LOUISE
Base elevation: 1,645m (5,396ft)
Summit: 2,637m (8,657ft)
Vertical: 1,000m (3,254ft)
Lifts: 2 quads, 2 triples, 4 doubles and 3 surface
50 runs: 25% beginner, 45% intermediate, 30% advanced
Average snowfall: 365cm (12ft)

Contacts
Information and reservations: ☎ 403-256-8473 (Calgary), 403-522-3555 (Banff National Park) or ☎ 1-800-258-7669
Banff/Lake Louise Central Reservations: ☎ 1-800-661-1676 or ☎ 403-760-5200
Snow phone: ☎ 403-244-6665
Home page: www.skilouise.com

Lake Louise – Front Side/South Face

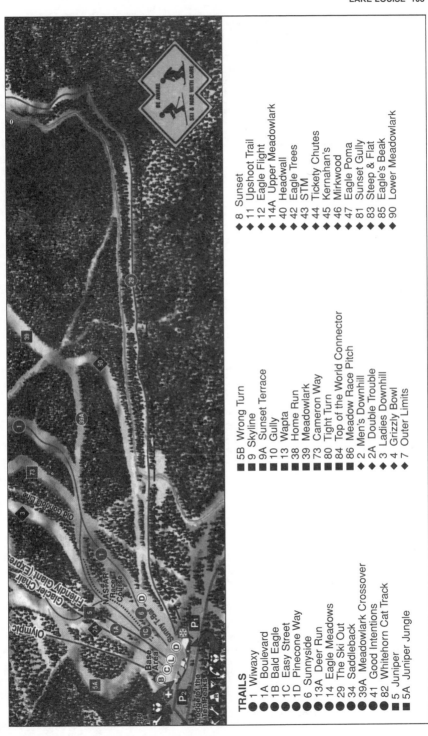

TRAILS

● 1 Wiwaxy
● 1A Boulevard
● 1B Bald Eagle
● 1C Easy Street
● 1D Pinecone Way
● 6 Sunnyside
● 13A Deer Run
● 14 Eagle Meadows
● 29 The Ski Out
● 34 Saddleback
● 39A Meadowlark Crossover
● 41 Good Intentions
● 82 Whitehorn Cat Track
■ 5 Juniper
■ 5A Juniper Jungle

■ 5B Wrong Turn
■ 9 Skyline
■ 9A Sunset Terrace
■ 10 Gully
■ 13 Wapta
■ 38 Home Run
■ 39 Meadowlark
■ 73 Cameron Way
■ 80 Tight Turn
■ 84 Top of the World Connector
■ 86 Meadow Race Pitch
◆ 2 Men's Downhill
◆ 2A Double Trouble
◆ 3 Ladies Downhill
◆ 4 Grizzly Bowl
◆ 7 Outer Limits

◆ 8 Sunset
◆ 11 Upshoot Trail
◆ 12 Eagle Flight
◆ 14A Upper Meadowlark
◆ 40 Headwall
◆ 42 Eagle Trees
◆ 43 STM
◆ 44 Tickety Chutes
◆ 45 Kernahan's
◆ 46 Mirkwood
◆ 47 Eagle Poma
◆ 81 Sunset Gully
◆ 83 Steep & Flat
◆ 85 Eagle's Beak
◆ 90 Lower Meadowlark

Lake Louise – Ptarmigan Paradise and Back Bowls

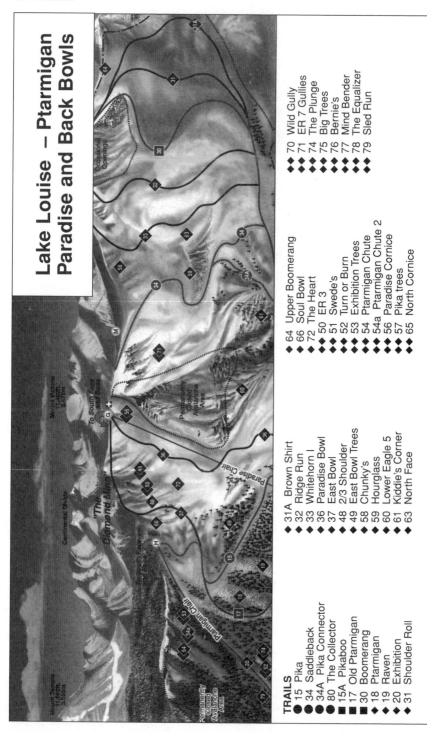

TRAILS

- ● 15 Pika
- ●● 34 Saddleback
- ●● 34A Pika Connector
- ●● 80 The Collector
- ■ 15A Pikaboo
- ■ 17 Old Ptarmigan
- ■ 30 Boomerang
- ◆ 18 Ptarmigan
- ◆ 19 Raven
- ◆ 20 Exhibition
- ◆ 31 Shoulder Roll

- ◆ 31A Brown Shirt
- ◆ 32 Ridge Run
- ◆ 33 Whitehorn I
- ◆ 36 Paradise Bowl
- ◆ 37 East Bowl
- ◆ 48 2/3 Shoulder
- ◆ 49 East Bowl Trees
- ◆ 58 Chunky's
- ◆ 59 Hourglass
- ◆ 60 Lower Eagle 5
- ◆ 61 Kiddie's Corner
- ◆ 63 North Face

- ◆ 64 Upper Boomerang
- ◆ 66 Soul Bowl
- ◆ 72 The Heart
- ◆ 50 ER 3
- ◆ 51 Swede's
- ◆ 52 Turn or Burn
- ◆ 53 Exhibition Trees
- ◆ 54 Ptarmigan Chute
- ◆ 54a Ptarmigan Chute 2
- ◆ 56 Paradise Cornice
- ◆ 57 Pika trees
- ◆ 65 North Cornice

- ◆ 70 Wild Gully
- ◆ 71 ER 7 Gullies
- ◆ 74 The Plunge
- ◆ 75 Big Trees
- ◆ 76 Bernie's
- ◆ 77 Mind Bender
- ◆ 78 The Equalizer
- ◆ 79 Sled Run

Lake Louise Larch Area

TRACKS

● 22 Marmot
● 28 Lookout
● 29 The Ski Out
■ 23 Wolverine
■ 25 Larch
■ 26 Larch Poma
■ 27 Bobcat
■ 66 Rock Garden

■ 87 Larch Link
◆ 24 Lynx
◆ 68 Lipalian Chute
◆ 89 Ford Hill Pitch
◆ 67 Elevator Shaft
◆ 69 Lookout Chutes
◆◆ 88 Tower 12

Purple Bowl
"Home of the Canadian Freestyle Championships"

Permanently Closed Avalanche Area

Larch Chair

Proposed Wolverine Ridge Lift and Trails

Temple Lodge
6,608ft.
2,015m

mogul fans. There is a large bowl on the back side of the summit that sometimes has powder and is a real pleasure for intermediate skiers (but only on a nice day). The Larch area on the far side is loved by intermediate skiers and boarders who like to walk above the lifts for powder. If you'd like to take the slow way around to the front, there is an eight kilometre, extremely gentle, ski-out.

The snow can be somewhat variable and the front is the first area to lose it come spring. Fortunately Louise has fairly extensive snowmaking, but this doesn't stop the snow from becoming crusty.

Overall Louise is an excellent destination. The promotional material states that you won't ski the same run twice which is a genuine possibility. The mountain is ideal for groups with varied abilities as it is easy to try different runs while meeting up at the same lift, or at one of the three lodges.

Cross-country
There are over 90 kilometres of groomed tracks and an almost incalculable number of options for back-country adventures. Keep in mind however that the Lake Louise area is in the heart of the Rockies and avalanches are not unusual. Skiing across and around the frozen lake is easy and a great way to enjoy the spectacular views.

Snowboarding
Boarders are certainly welcome all over the hill, though Louise hasn't developed the same sort of boarding culture as at other hills in the Rockies. Nonetheless there is a half-pipe near the base of the Summit Platter lift and the trees on the back can harbour some good soft snow. Unfortunately the snow *can* be a bit crusty on much of the mountain which is always a great frustration to boarders.

Lessons and rentals
Group lessons start at $25 per person for 1½ hours. Private lessons are high at twice that price, though may be an option if you arrange your own group. Ski school for kids is available and starts at $19 per hour; day-care/lesson is on offer from $27. Babies can be minded for $20 a day, or $4 per hour.

Ski, pole and boot rental starts from around $17.

Lift tickets
	Adult	Senior (65+)/Student (16-25 with an ID card)	Child (6-12)
Full day	$43	$33.65	$14
Half day	$33.54	$27.10	$14

Multi-day passes can help reduce costs and the $49 Louise Plus Card reduces tickets by $12 a day.

Getting there and around
Lake Louise is just on the Alberta side of the Great Divide, at the extreme eastern edge of the Bow Valley. The lake, Château and other hotels and services that make up the tiny community are separated from the ski field by the Trans-Canada. Because the ski area is comprised of three faces, there are runs facing most points of the compass.

If you're coming from Calgary, the closest city, Lake Louise is a 2¼ hour drive due west. Count on about 45 minutes from Banff. When you reach the Louise junction, the skiing is two kilometres to the north and the village is just on the south side of the highway. The Lake and the Château are another four kilometres up hill. There is a shuttle from the hotels to the slopes and a snow shuttle runs from Calgary for day skiers.

Accommodation

There is no accommodation right on the slopes, however there are some great options around Lake Louise.

The *Youth Hostel* (☎ 403-522-2200) in the village is the best budget option, with dorm beds at $19.55. Ask about their ski packages.

The *Château* (☎ 403-522-3511 or CP Reservations ☎ 1-800-441-1414) becomes a much more viable choice during the winter months as the prices come way down. They start around $115, however most rooms are above the $200 mark and climb from there. Close to the Château is the TV-less *Deer Lodge* (☎ 403-522-3747 or ☎ 1-800-661-1595) with rooms from around $100. Down by the village *Lake Louise Inn* (☎ 403-522-3791 or ☎ 1-800-661-9237) has rooms from round $80.

If everywhere is full at Lake Louise itself, or if you fancy a bit more action, Banff is always a fair alternative. For further information contact Banff/Lake Louise Central Reservations ☎ 1-800-661 1676 or ☎ 403-760-5200.

Après ski

The base lodge is being rebuilt and expanded and has a cafeteria and lounge equipped with a fireplace, though you'll feel lonely quite early as Calgarians tend to head for home. The Château has a good bar as well as several lounges, all of which serve food. The *Poppy Room* is the only place for breakfast in the winter and is popular with families. All the hotels have restaurants and there is a deli, coffee shop and small grocer down in the village.

CANMORE NORDIC CENTRE

Located just above the town of Canmore, ten minutes from the Banff Park Gates, the Nordic Centre is one of Canada's premier cross-country venues. This fantastic facility was established and built for the 1988 Winter Olympics and continues to be maintained publicly although there is now a small charge for a visit.

The Nordic centre is a mecca for Canada's best cross-country skiers and bi-athletes; international competitions are common. The centre even has some snowmaking! Runs are available for literally all abilities and are well marked. Perhaps the only potential drawback to the area is its propensity to become quite icy.

Should you get tired of the crowds, which are not too heavy, or you feel like some un-groomed tracks, drive further up Spray Lakes Rd (a gravel road) where you'll find some great back-country skiing. At the top of the hill you will see parking for Goat's Creek Trail – this offers a beautiful 18km trail all the way to Banff.

Spray Lakes Rd can be a bit difficult during a heavy winter, but does continue all the way around to Peter Lougheed Provincial Park and consequently Kananaskis Country. **Information and reservations**: ☎ 403-678-2400

Lessons and rentals

Expect to pay $20 for 1½ hour group lessons in classical or skating basics. Private lessons are $40 for the first hour and $20 for additional people. Multi-week lessons are available for adults and kids as well as instructor courses.

Rentals can be had all day or for two hours and a regular package goes for $22 for the day. Children's skis and boots are $13. For a change, why not rent some snowshoes ($13 a day).

Accommodation

There is no accommodation right at the Nordic Centre but the town of Canmore is becoming a significant alternative to Banff. Either town affords convenient access to the mountains. The number of hotels continues to expand in Canmore and there is a wide selection of friendly and welcoming B&Bs with rooms from around $65. During the winter months most places have space so it's worth calling into the Travel Alberta office (☎ 403-678-5277 or ☎ 1-800-661-8888) to pick up a list; the office is located just off the Trans-Canada at the western edge of Canmore.

Canmore has a few less expensive motels. *Akai Motel* (☎ 403-678-4664) has rooms from $43. Moving to the mid-range ($80-$150) there is a wide selection. Places to consider include: *The Georgetown Inn* (☎ 403-678-3439 or ☎ 1-800-657-5955) which has a distinctly British feel; *Best Western Green Gables Inn* (☎ 403-678-5488 or ☎ 1-800-661-2133); or *Quality Resort Château Canmore* (☎ 403-678-6699 or ☎ 1-800-228-5151) which is an impressive new hotel.

Après ski
As cross-country skiers are keenly aware, their sport does not trap them in one place, nor do they necessarily feel as though they need to ski all day to get their money's worth. After a few good hours at the Nordic Centre it is well worth going down to Canmore to have lunch at one of the great pubs or restaurants along Main Street. There is a cafeteria at the Nordic Centre and several picnic spots along the many runs.

Jasper

Jasper is the other town in the Alberta Rockies and is much like Banff was twenty years ago. With roughly 4,500 permanent residents it is a rather sleepy mountain town – especially during winter. Jasper attracts thousands of skiers and hikers from Edmonton, as well as those who come across Canada by train. It has also become an obligatory stop for coach tours during the summer season. Although Jasper is north of Banff, it is about one thousand feet (300m) lower in elevation thereby maintaining a relatively mild climate.

Regular visitors tend to remain faithful to either Banff or Jasper, with Jasper slowly winning more and more converts as Banff becomes an ever busier international resort. Because Jasper is still a major changing area for Canadian National trains, the town retains its working class feel and close-knit community. Jasper certainly derives much of its income from tourism and the hotel workforce is often transient, but perhaps as a result of Jasper's relative isolation, the community is more than just a resort.

As a national park, all wildlife is protected. Should you not encounter the elusive elk you are either not in Jasper or are visually impaired! The area is rife with moose and come spring, bears are a common sight around town. Regular precautions, like not petting the wildlife, are essential.

Skiing
The closest downhill skiing is at Marmot Basin, just minutes from the town. There is plenty of excellent cross-country around the town, as well as east towards Edmonton, and especially south along the Jasper Parkway. The treed area east of the railway track which shelters Jasper Park Lodge is a convenient area for a couple of hours of cross-country. Skis can be rented in town and at many hotels. Keep in mind that while skiing cross-country you will encounter wild animals.

❑ **JASPER – TOURIST INFORMATION**

Jasper Tourism
632 Connaught Drive
Jasper TOE 1EO
☎ 403-852-3858 or ☎ 1-800-473-8135

Jasper National Park
(address as Jasper Tourism)
☎ 403-852-6162

Getting there and around

Jasper is four hours' drive from Banff and three hours from Lake Louise via the sometimes impassable Jasper Parkway (# 93). From Edmonton, Jasper is a 4½ hour drive and from Kamloops in central BC it is about five hours up the Yellowhead highway. Greyhound of course provides a service, but the most romantic way to arrive from east or west is by Via Rail (☎ 1-800-561-8630).

Once in Jasper you would have to be in fairly bad shape not to be able to walk everywhere. However there is a local taxi service and Marmot Basin has a shuttle service. If you are wealthy enough to stay in *Jasper Park Lodge* they would be more than happy to drive you in and out of town.

MARMOT BASIN

Marmot is probably the least busy of the resorts in the Rocky Mountain parks and, like the adjacent town of Jasper, offers a quiet alternative to Banff. One of the great pleasures of skiing Marmot is the absolute lack of lift lines – even during the busy Christmas/New Year season five minutes is a long wait. The mountain itself is a nice combination of cut runs and a large bowl well above the tree line, so when the snow is plentiful, strong skiers want to climb as high as possible.

Marmot doesn't make snow and the grooming methods are traditional with no preservatives or hardeners. This means that seasons can vary extensively so it's worth checking snow conditions before going. If Marmot is having a good season head for the upper bowl and then all the way down through Eagle East. The quad offers access to most of the beginner runs and the triple chair is for those who love bumps. Intermediates get the middle of the mountain.

Cross country

Although cross-country skiing is not possible right at the hill there are plenty of tracks in Jasper. Visit the Park Information Centre in the middle of town for maps and ideas.

Snowboarding

Marmot has a new park for boards and a good enough lift system to avoid too much walking. The upper bowl is great after a large snowfall.

Lessons and rentals

Group lessons cost $24 (two hours) for anyone over 13, (Junior, $16; Tiny Tot (4-6), $20); the private version is $45 per hour. Adult ski improvement weeks cost $96; a 'week' includes ten hours of lessons, a video night and a night out in Jasper. Never Before inclusive packages (lift ticket, two-hour lesson and equipment rental) are $39 on skis and $45 for boarders.

❏ MARMOT BASIN

Base elevation: 1,700m (5,440ft)
Summit: 2,601m (8,534ft)
Vertical: 897m (2,944ft)
Lifts: 1 quad, 1 triple, 3 doubles and 3 surface (2 T-bars and 1 handle tow)
53 runs: 35% beginner, 35% intermediate, 30% advanced
Average snowfall: 400cm
Lift operating hours: 9am-4.30pm

Contacts
Information and reservations: ☎ 403-852-3816
Snow phone: ☎ 403-488-5909
Home page: www.skimarmot.com

Marmot Basin

TRAILS

- ● 1 Home Run
- ● 2 School House
- ● 3 Slow Poke
- ● 11 Sleepy Hollow
- ● 12 Old Road
- ● 13 Triple Access
- ● 14 Bunny Hop
- ● 15 Power Line
- ● 17 Wallow Traverse
- ● 31 S-Turn
- ● 33 Basin Run
- ■ 4 Upper Access
- ■ 10 Tranquiliser
- ■ 16 Show Off
- ■ 18 Wilverine Wallow
- ■ 19 Willi's Way
- ■ 25 Show Off Cat Track
- ■ 28 Punch Bowl
- ■ 29 Paradise
- ■ 30 Marmot Run
- ■ 32 Gun Sight
- ■ 39 Knob Traverse
- ■ 47 High Trail
- ■ 48 Chalet Express
- ■ 49 Eagle Flight
- ◆ 5 Rock Gardens
- ◆ 6 Slash
- ◆ 7 Spillway
- ◆ 8 Lift Line
- ◆ 9 Dromedary
- ◆ 20 Exhibition
- ◆ 21 Kiefer's Dream
- ◆ 22 Caribou Knoll
- ◆ 23 Kiefer's Chute
- ◆ 24 Geikie Street
- ◆ 26 Highway 16
- ◆ 27 Milk Run
- ◆ 34 Party Slope
- ◆ 35 Knob Bowl
- ◆ 36 Knob Hill
- ◆ 37 Dupres Bowl
- ◆ 38 Dupres Chutes
- ◆ 40 Upper Basin
- ◆ 41 Peak Run
- ◆ 42 McCready's Choice
- ◆ 43 High Traverse
- ◆ 44 Ridge Run
- ◆ 45 Thunder Bowl
- ◆ 46 Chalet Slope
- ◆ 50 Charlie's Bowl
- ◆ 51 Expressway
- ◆ 52 Eagle East
- ◆ 53 Wendy's Choice

LIFTS
A Eagle Express quad chairlift
B Tranquilizer chairlift
C School House T-Bar
D Caribou chairlift
E Triple chairlift
F Kiefer T-Bar
G Knob chairlift
H Handle Tow

OTHERS
1 Caribou Chalet
2 Little Rascals nursery
3 Ski patrol
4 Caribou ticket sales
5 Public safety centre
6 Eagle Chalet
7 Paradise Chalet
8 Ski patrol

Lift tickets

	Adult	Youth (13-17*)	Senior (65+)	Junior (6-12)
Full day	$39	$33	$28	$17
Five day	$195	$165	$140	$85

* Students up to 25 years old with an ID can also have a youth discount. Children aged 5 and under ski free.

You should only have to pay these prices during the high season – mid-December to mid-January and February to April. Discounts apply most other times.

Getting there and around

Marmot is 19km from Jasper town; however a day trip from anywhere else is almost impossible. Fortunately Jasper is a great place to spend a few days. Greyhound has daily services to Jasper from Edmonton, Kamloops, Vancouver and Prince George. A Ski Area Shuttle bus operates between hotels in Jasper and Marmot.

Accommodation

There is no accommodation on-site but Jasper is just 16 kilometres away. As Jasper is smaller and quieter than Banff there is a little less choice, however prices are generally lower and beds are easy to find during winter with the exception of the Christmas/New Year period. The following are just a few of the options; many other guest houses are available – for details contact Jasper Tourism (☎ 403-852-3858 or ☎ 1-800-473-8135).

Jasper's best and most attractive hotel, *Jasper Park Lodge* (☎ 403-852-3301 or ☎ 1-800-441-1414), was built by Canadian National Railway. Although not grand like Banff Springs or Château Frontinac, Jasper Park Lodge is first class with many superbly equipped chalets dotted through the woods. Ski packages which include a shuttle to Marmot start from $156 per person based on a two-room unit for two days. Prices are discounted between the end of November and mid-December.

Central Jasper has the *Astoria Hotel* (☎ 403-852-3351 or ☎ 1-800-661-7343) with packages from $128. *Athabasca Hotel* (☎ 403-852-3386 or ☎ 1-800-563-9859) with its lively pub has inclusive deals from $112.

Just slightly further out is the good *Lobstick Lodge* (☎ 403-852-4471 or ☎ 1-800-661-9317) and a couple of other hotels run by the same company. The short walk into town often involves crossing the street to avoid elk! Packages are from $156 per person.

There are several youth hostels in the park area; *Whistler's Mountain Hostel* (☎ 403-439-3139) is the only one that remains open all winter.

Après ski

Marmot has a new chalet at its base with shops, a café, a lounge and a full-service restaurant.

Jasper has everything else with several fun pubs and restaurants. Walking along the main street and one street back covers much of the action. Call into *Papa George's* for a good meal or even the pizzeria next door. *Tokyo Tom's* has real(ish) Japanese food.

❏ Parks
Canada has literally hundreds of National and Provincial Parks and even a few World Heritage Parks. While the Americans were the first to create a nationally protected area, the young Canadian government came around to the idea in 1885 and created Rocky Mountains National Park. The area was later split up for administrative reasons and became Banff, Jasper and Yoho National Parks.

Kananaskis Country

A mere hour west of Calgary, Kananaskis Country Provincial Park is considered one of the most beautiful and accessible parks in western Canada. The park area is easily reached via #40 off the Trans-Canada, but can also be arrived at via the unsealed route #742 along Spray Lakes Smith-Dorian highway, above Canmore. Another route runs near the hamlet of Bragg Creek, although the unsealed connection to the main valley is closed in winter.

The far end of Kananaskis becomes **Peter Lougheed Provincial Park** with even fewer people and a couple of camping sites (Reservations ☎ 403-591-7226) with hot water. The snow tends to be better in this area.

Skiing Kananaskis Country
The two principal hills are 'friendly' Fortress Mountain and Nakiska which was built for the 1988 Winter Olympics. There was a fair amount of environmental controversy surrounding the construction of Nakiska at Mount Allan and as a result of protection there will likely be minimal further development in the valley. For the time being the park's main valley has one world-class golf course, the two ski areas and a small, de luxe village along with the standard administration and information services.

There is a significant amount of cross-country skiing throughout the valley including several multi-day treks. Hundreds of kilometres of trails lead out from the village area and further up the valley a multitude of more difficult back-country adventures can be found. Pick up a map from the Park Information office (☎ 403-591-7555, Kananaskis Village, BOX 249, TOL 2H0) in the centre of town. **It is imperative that you check the avalanche status before setting out.**

Kananaskis Village
The village at Kananaskis is a first-class facility with three excellent hotels and great food to go with the views. This is a great area to relax and the views on a clear day are spectacular. Canadian Pacific's *Lodge at Kananaskis* (☎ 403-591-7711 or ☎ 1-800-441-1414) is a superb lodge and hotel with all the amenities – some rooms even have fireplaces. Doubles start from $210 and climb rapidly. The *Fireside Lounge* has the best Caesar salads in Alberta!

A slightly less expensive option is the still excellent *Best Western Kananaskis Inn* (☎ 403-591-7500 or ☎ 1-800-528-1234) with doubles starting from $140.

For information about the various packages available and for reservations phone ☎ 1-800-258-7669.

❏ **Western Cordillera**
This is the magnificent range of mountains which extend from the top of Alaska and down the western coast of the Americas all the way to Tierra Del Fuego at the bottom of Chile and Argentina. Often in Canada these mountains are referred to simply as the Rockies, whereas in reality, between Alberta and Vancouver Island there are five major and distinct ranges that can themselves be sub-divided. The Rocky Mountains are the most easterly range that straddle the Great Divide and consequently the Alberta-BC border. Heading west from the Rockies, the three central ranges are the Purcell, Selkirk and Monashee. Furthest west are the Coastal Mountains. The highest mountain in the BC Rockies is Mount Robson on the western side of the range, reaching 12,972ft (3891.6m).

NAKISKA

Nakiska was conceived and developed for the 1988 Winter Olympics and is fortunate to be just one hour from Calgary which was the reason for its development. As a show resort it is very hi-tech with fantastic high-speed quads, a nice lodge and the nearby Kananaskis Village with the only real hotels in the park. Nakiska is a mountain for cruisers; its long, fairly smooth, steep runs – just the kind you would imagine down-hill racers to be flying down – are particularly ideal for intermediates. Unfortunately there is not a great deal of variety, but Nakiska is a good for those whose knees are a bit tired of bumps.

The eternal problem with Mount Allan, on which Nakiska rests, is the tragic lack of natural snow. But, as a result of Olympic money, the resort has 85% snowmaking. This is not a mountain for powder fans, but may yet be the training ground for future gold medallists.

The two great quads provide long, fast runs while the slower Gold chair accesses steeper inclines. While the majority of the mountain is rated intermediate, many improving beginners can enjoy longer runs than they might elsewhere.

Snowboarding

There is a half-pipe near the top of the Silver chair, but the crusty, groomed runs have not made this a mecca for boarders. Nevertheless, Nakiska is a great place to learn and to try a little speed.

Cross country

The area has offers all sorts of trails; tours for groups of five or more can be arranged through the main lodge.

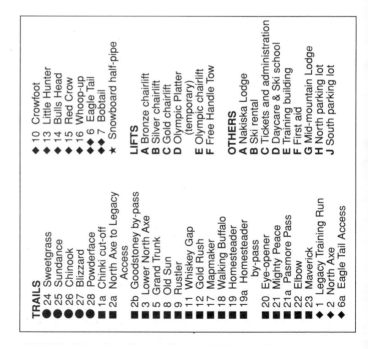

TRAILS
- ● 24 Sweetgrass
- ● 25 Sundance
- ● 26 Chinook
- ● 27 Blizzard
- ● 28 Powderface
- ■ 1a Chinki cut-off
- ■ 2a North Axe to Legacy Access
- ■ 2b Goodstoney by-pass
- ■ 3 Lower North Axe
- ■ 5 Grand Trunk
- ■ 8 Old Sun
- ■ 9 Rustler
- ■ 11 Whiskey Gap
- ■ 12 Gold Rush
- ■ 17 Mapmaker
- ■ 18 Walking Buffalo
- ■ 19 Homesteader
- ■ 19a Homesteader by-pass
- ■ 20 Eye-opener
- ■ 21 Mighty Peace
- ■ 21a Pasmore Pass
- ■ 22 Elbow
- ■ 23 Maverick
- ♦ 1 Legacy Training Run
- ♦ 2 North Axe
- ♦ 6a Eagle Tail Access
- ♦ 10 Crowfoot
- ♦ 13 Little Hunter
- ♦ 14 Bulls Head
- ♦ 15 Red Crow
- ♦ 16 Whoop-up
- ♦ 6 Eagle Tail
- ♦ 7 Bobtail
- ★ Snowboard half-pipe

LIFTS
- A Bronze chairlift
- B Silver chairlift
- C Gold chairlift
- D Olympic Platter (temporary)
- E Olympic chairlift
- F Free Handle Tow

OTHERS
- A Nakiska Lodge
- B Ski rental
- C Tickets and administration
- D Daycare & Ski school
- E Training building
- F First aid
- G Mid-mountain Lodge
- H North parking lot
- J South parking lot

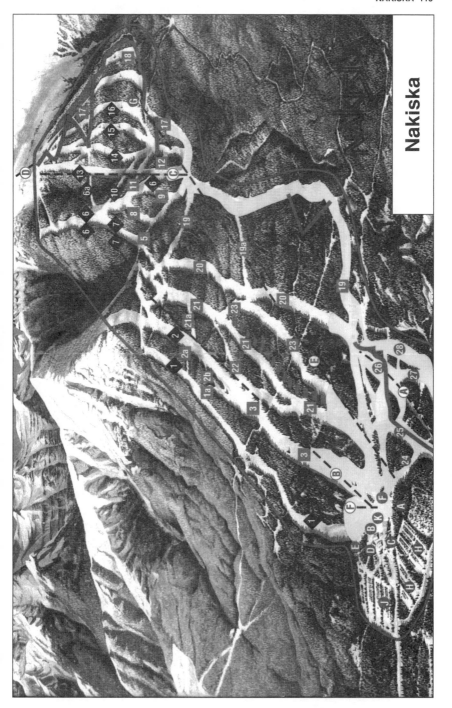

Nakiska

❑ **NAKISKA**
Base elevation: 1,525m (5,003ft)
Summit: 2,260 (7,412ft)
Vertical: 735m (2,412ft)
Lifts: 2 quads, 1 triple, 1 double, 1 surface
28 Runs: 16% beginner, 70% intermediate, 14% advanced, also 35 acre of gladed terrain
Average snowfall: 250cm (98in) and plenty of snowmaking
Lift operating hours: 9am-4pm

Contacts
Information and reservations: ☎ 403-591-7777
Snow phone ☎ 403-244-6665
Home page: www.skilouise.com

Lessons and rentals

It's easy to rent equipment around the lodge area; like Fortress further up the valley, Nakiska has a reputation as a good place to learn to ski.

Basic lessons start from $20 per hour.

Lift tickets

	Adult	Youth/Student/Senior	Child (6-12)
Full Day	$36	$29	$15
Half day (12noon)	$29	$25	$15
From 2pm	$20	$20	$10

Skiing is free for children aged 5 and under.
Tickets are also valid at Fortress 30 minutes up the valley.

Getting there and around

Just an hour west of Calgary, Nakiska rises above Kananaskis village. Since there is no public transport to Nakiska you will need to drive.

Accommodation and après ski

All the accommodation is at the nearby Kananaskis village; the village has a rather mature feel and with the beautiful surroundings it is a wonderful place for a romantic weekend.

FORTRESS MOUNTAIN

Fortress Mountain is one of those hills that's known by everyone locally and almost no one further afield. This is partly due to its location at the far end of Kananaskis Provincial Park, well off any major route. What this does mean is that a trip to Fortress will unfold the spectacular Kananaskis for you; the views around the ski area can be stunning.

Fortress is less developed and more isolated than other resorts in the Rockies. It also lacks the almost compulsory high-speed quad. Nonetheless lift tickets are a little

❑ **Multi-mountain passes**
The new move in marketing seems to be towards multi-mountain passes. The biggest winners so far are skiers along the Alberta-BC border who can now ski eight resorts all season for around $900. The ticket includes Lake Louise, Fernie, Mt Norquay, Wintergreen, Fortress, Nakiska, Panorama and Marmot Basin.

cheaper and if there is an abundance of their well-promoted dry powder a great day out can be had. The bumps off the Canadian triple chair are always good fun and the less developed far side can offer some good all round exploring. On a good day this is where the powder will be but watch the ground closely as there can some hidden rocks or baby trees.

If you're tired of skiing and would like some spectator action, you may be able to see some Canadian free-stylers training close to the lodge. Fortress is also promoting cat-skiing – a more affordable alternative to heli-skiing.

Snowboarding
Boarders have been welcome here since the sport came to Canada and after a decent snowfall the area becomes quite popular. Many Calgarians go to Fortress to improve their skills.

Cross country
Kananaskis is literally full of great tracks for all abilities. Stop off at the Park Information Office. Avalanches have recently claimed lives here so all the necessary precautions should be taken.

Lessons and rentals
Group lessons for both skiing and snowboarding are available from $45 a day for three hours or $25 for 1 1/2 hours. Private lessons are $40 per hour. Day care is also available.

Lift tickets
	Adult	Youth/Student/Senior	Child (6-12)
Full day	$32	$25	$18
Half day	$25	$20	$15
After 2pm	$18	$12	$10

Children aged 5 and under ski free. Day tickets may also be used at Nakiska on the same day.

Getting there and around
To get to Fortress you'll need a car. The resort is a little less than 1 1/2 hours from Calgary. Coming west on the Trans-Canada you turn south on the #40 just before entering the mountains; continue up the valley until the Fortress turn off where you'll slowly climb up the gravel road to the highest base elevation of any resort in Canada!

Accommodation
There is limited accommodation on the hill but it is affordable with dorm beds for around $20. There are also a few roomy chalets which can sleep up to 10 people for $150+ per night. For information and reservations phone ☎ 403-591-7108. Otherwise rooms are in the more luxurious Kananaskis Village or Calgary.

❏ Dog Sledding and Ski-Joring
Not only is Dog Sledding an interesting and involved sport, but its roots in Canada are genuine. Whereas today roads, air and snowmobiles are the preferred forms of winter travel, early settlers and trappers often travelled great distances with their dogs. Races are common throughout the north and the greatest of all is the famous 1,770km Iditarod Trail sled dog race in Alaska. Many Sled tours operate in the Rockies and the town of Canmore hosts an international competition annually at the end of January.

The Norwegian version of dog sledding, which has been imported to Canada, involves a cross-country skier being pulled by one to three of man's best friends. At least Ski-Joring doesn't involve keeping upwards of 30 dogs.

Fortress Mountain

Cat Skiing Area →

← Cat Skiing Area

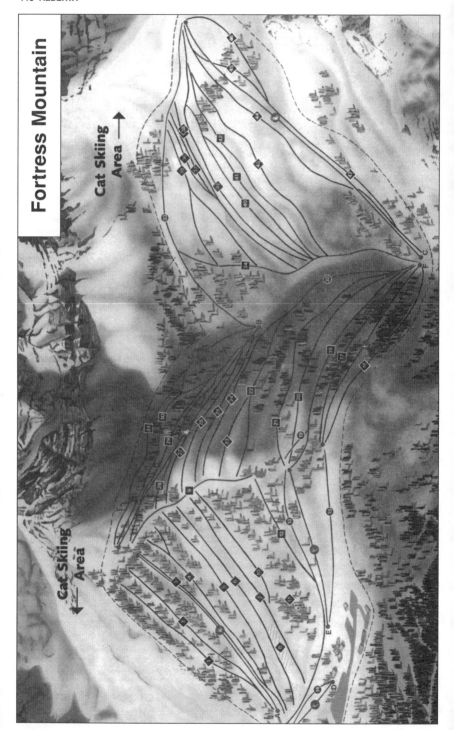

TRAILS
- ● 13 Garden Path
- ● 14 Courtyard
- ● 15 Sloe Gin
- ● 19 Rookie Traverse
- ● 32 Easy Out
- ● 33 Canterbury Trial
- ■ 9 Ridge
- ■ 12 Raceway
- ■ 17 Turkish Delight
- ■ 18 Rookie
- ■ 20 Palisade
- ■ 21 Big Scoop
- ■ 22 Sorcerer
- ■ 28 Show Off
- ■ 29 Enchanted Forest
- ■ 30 Roller Coaster
- ■ 31 Wall Street
- ■ 34 Jolly Jester
- ■ 40 Taint
- ■ 41 Getaway
- ■ 42 Pitchfork
- ♦ 1 Friar's Tuck
- ♦ 2 Palisade Park
- ♦ 3 Watch Me
- ♦ 4 Portcullis
- ♦ 5 1st Chute
- ♦ 6 2nd Chute
- ♦ 7 3rd Chute
- ♦ 8 Half Pipe
- ♦ 10 4th Chute
- ♦ 11 Aerial Site
- ♦ 16 Rampart
- ♦ 23 Backside Glades
- ♦ 24 Burnt Out
- ♦ 25 Tight Pride 2
- ♦ 26 Tight Pride 1
- ♦ 27 Harry's
- ♦ 35 Glades
- ♦ 36 Damian
- ♦ 37 Lucifers
- ♦ 38 Devils Gulch
- ♦ 39 New Getaway
- ♦ 43 Flying Fortress
- ♦ 44 Good Knight
- ♦ 45 Coliseum
- ♦ 46 Cauldron
- ♦ 47 Sherwood Forest

LIFTS
- A The Canadian triple chairlift
- B Backside double chairlift
- C Farside double chairlift
- D Beginner's T-Bar
- E Curved T-Bar South
- F Curved T-Bar North

❏ FORTRESS MOUNTAIN
Base elevation: 2,040m (6,692ft)
Summit: 2,369m (7,775ft)
Vertical: 329m (1,089ft)
Lifts: 1 triple, 2 doubles, 3 surface (cat-skiing also available February to April)
47 Runs: 6 beginner, 15 intermediate, 26 advanced
Average snowfall: 630cm (21ft)
Lift operating hours: 9am-4pm Monday to Friday, 8.30am-4pm Saturday and Sunday

Contacts
Information and reservations: ☎ 403-591-7108
Snow phone: ☎ 403-244-6665

Après ski
Hmmm! There is a bar at the hill but little else – a nice quiet spot! A stay at Fortress can still be good fun though, with its friendly, relaxed atmosphere. The budget accommodation attracts younger people so the parties can be quite lively during holiday seasons.

CASTLE MOUNTAIN RESORT

This is a friendly little place in a beautiful setting which is well worth keeping an eye on as they are in the process of upgrading their lift system and adding 700 acres of new terrain! This expansion should help to move Castle closer to the major resort category. For the moment this southern Alberta hill is not particularly well known and is off major routes though in reality Castle is not hard to visit. It's a good place to start for some dry Rockies powder, before heading on to the first-class resorts of southern BC.

A new trail rating system based on a range from 1 to 10, with 10 being the most difficult is being tried here. This system is more precise than the traditional three or four level scale, but having that many colours has to be more confusing. For the moment Castle has a good variety of runs for all abilities. Once the expansion is complete the hill should have all sorts of good open skiing above the trees. For information and reservations phone ☎ 403-627-5101.

Snowboarding
Boards are welcome and if there is a good dumping of powder it's worth heading into the steep treed area.

Cross country
On the drive into the resort there are several marked spots for cross country including a provincial park.

Lessons and rentals
Because Castle promotes itself as a family resort there are a great variety of lesson options. Discover Skiing all-day packages cost $26 and the boarding version is $38. Group lessons are $19, or $13 each for three or more people.

Rental packages are around $17 ($27 for boards) per day.

Lift tickets
	Adult	Junior (13-18)	Child (7-12)
Full day	$29	$22	$13
Half day	$21	$16	$9

Students also receive discounts and affordable family passes are available.

Getting there and around
Castle mountain is in southern Alberta close to the BC border at the very end of the #774 secondary road. The last third of the trip is not paved, though it's not too steep. Watch for ice! The closest town to the hill is **Pincher Creek** located 45 minutes east. Otherwise Castle is about the same distance from Crowsnest and about 2½ hours south of Calgary.

Accommodation and après ski
None. The lodge is being expanded and you can have some food and a beer here , but the closest beds are in Pincher Creek. There are some great B&Bs in the area with good prices. Call the Reservations office (☎ 403-627-5101) for more details. Hotels in Pincher Creek are rarely full in the winter and a good double can be obtained for $80.

❏ CASTLE MOUNTAIN
Base elevation: 1,310m (4,300ft)
Vertical: Will increase to 823m (2,700ft)
Lifts: 1 triple, 3 surface
Projected run breakdown: 15% Novice, 55% intermediate, 30% Expert
Average snowfall: N/A

Castle Mountain Resort

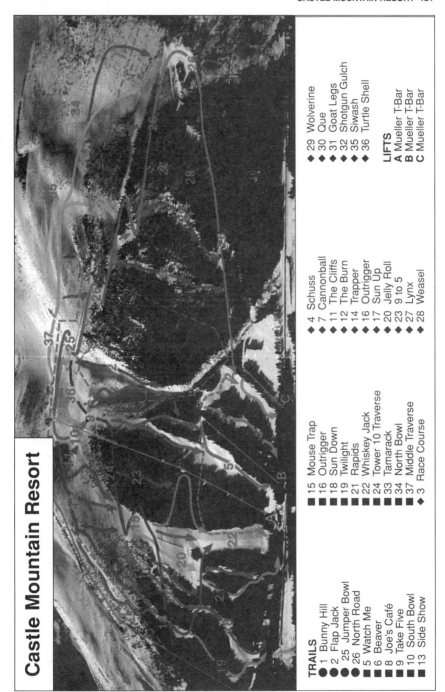

TRAILS
- 1 Bunny Hill
- 2 Flap Jack
- 25 Jumper Bowl
- 26 North Road
- 5 Watch Me
- 6 Beaver
- 8 Joe's Café
- 9 Take Five
- 10 South Bowl
- 13 Side Show

- 15 Mouse Trap
- 16 Outrigger
- 18 Sun Down
- 19 Twilight
- 21 Rapids
- 22 Whiskey Jack
- 24 Tower 10 Traverse
- 33 Tamarack
- 34 North Bowl
- 37 Middle Traverse
- ◆ 3 Race Course

- ◆ 4 Schuss
- ◆ 7 Cannonball
- ◆ 11 The Cliffs
- ◆ 12 The Burn
- ◆ 14 Trapper
- ◆ 16 Outrigger
- ◆ 17 Sun Up
- ◆ 20 Jelly Roll
- 23 9 to 5
- ◆ 27 Lynx
- ◆ 28 Weasel

- ◆ 29 Wolverine
- ◆ 30 Que
- ◆ 31 Goat Legs
- ◆ 32 Shotgun Gulch
- ◆ 35 Siwash
- ◆ 36 Turtle Shell

LIFTS
- **A** Mueller T-Bar
- **B** Mueller T-Bar
- **C** Mueller T-Bar

PART 4: THE PRAIRIES

Skiing the Prairies

Moving east from the Rockies and Alberta, the world's second largest nation spreads out over the Great Plains meeting up with the rocky, lake-filled Canadian Shield. The majesty of this land is gentler than that of the western mountains or the dramatic east coast. However the region's beauty and genuine hospitality make Canada's centre well worth a visit.

The provinces of Saskatchewan and Manitoba along with Alberta are part of Canada's great agricultural backbone and indeed host a great deal more farmland than mountains so it's unlikely either province would be the first choice for an international skier. It would be unfair though to write either place off as unappealing winter destinations.

These provinces are almost entirely flat, but the landscape does undulate, mostly as a result of the coulees carved by the Prairies' many rivers. Needless to say this environment provides a great variety of cross-country opportunities and with abundant snowfalls, long treks through the valleys and forests of the Canadian Shield are available almost everywhere. The top third of Saskatchewan and over half of Manitoba consist of the forested and lake-covered shield which is both dramatic and relatively inaccessible. Many a snowmobiler hopes it remains that way.

Climate
A cold winter in the Canadian Prairies is guaranteed. Winnipeg has the distinction of being one of the world's coldest cities, with average daily highs for January below -13°C! There really is no area in either province which offers respite from winter which explains why so many locals retire to the west coast or further south. Winters in Saskatchewan are fairly dry which makes the cold somewhat more bearable and locals will attest to the beauty of the frozen land.

Getting around Saskatchewan and Manitoba
The northern areas of both provinces have few roads, whereas traversing the southern regions is easy. Perhaps the most touristed winter spot is Churchill, Manitoba – a popular place for seeing polar bears. As the roads are generally flat the greatest difficulty when driving can be finding the road beneath the blowing snow – prairie storms are some of the wildest in Canada. Bends in the road are usually the result of farms or towns rather than natural obstructions – in fact Saskatchewan is the only province in Canada with totally arbitrary borders.

Saskatoon and **Regina** both have regional airports; Winnipeg's is international.

❏ **TOURIST INFORMATION**
Tourism Saskatchewan
1919 Saskatchewan Drive
Regina, Saskatchewan, S4P3V7
☎ 306 787-2300 or ☎ 1-800-667-7191

Travel Manitoba
Dept 3083, 7th Floor
155 Carlton St, Winnipeg
Manitoba, R3C 3H8
☎ 204 942-2535 or ☎ 1-800-665-0040

Skiing Saskatchewan

Despite all the talk of farming there are some regional ski areas in both provinces; Saskatchewan even has two quads! This is also a good province in which to learn to ski, or indeed for those who suffer from vertigo!

Near Kamsack in eastern Saskatchewan is **Duck Mountain** (☎ 306-542-1111) with the longest run in the province at 1.6km. There are three surface lifts. **Duck Mountain Provincial Park** also has 70km of cross-country trails, 50km of which are groomed.

North-east of Moose Jaw, Buffalo Pound Provincial Park is home to **White Track Ski Area** (☎ 306-691-0100) with its three surface lifts. There is also cross-country in the park. **Blackstrap Ski Hill** (☎ 306-492-2400) in Blackstrap Provincial Park has a triple chair and a T-bar.

One of Saskatchewan's two quads is on **Ochapowace Mountain** (☎ 306-696-2522 or ☎ 1-800-668-6226) near Broadview in south-east Saskatchewan. One run is over one kilometre long.

Close to Melfort, north-east of Saskatoon, are **Keewatin Ski Resort** (☎ 306-275-2234) and **Wapiti Valley Regional Park** (☎ 306-862-5621) with two and three surface lifts respectively.

Near Fort Qu'Appelle is **Mission Ridge** (☎ 306-332-5479) with four surface lifts. **Cudworth Ski Area** (☎ 306-256-3281) has a rope-tow.

In south-west Saskatchewan near Stranraer is **Twin Towers Ski Area** (☎ 306-377-4551) with two surface lifts. Also in the south west, straddling the Alberta border, is the attractive **Cypress Hills Interprovincial Park** (☎ 306-662-4411) with 24km of groomed cross-country runs and a very interesting topography.

Timber Ridge (☎ 306-469-4545) near Big River has two surface lifts.

Saskatchewan's other quad at **Table Mountain** (☎ 306-937-2920) is just 18km west of Battleford. At present there are a quad and three surface lifts but more are likely to be constructed. There are three green runs and four blue; night skiing is possible three nights a week.

A great way to visit the northern part of Saskatchewan on cross-country skis (without having to fly) is on the 60km of tracks at **Lac La Ronge Provincial Park** (☎ 306-425-4234) some runs are lit at night.

Skiing Manitoba

Manitoba, the geographical centre of Canada, is an interesting and genuinely friendly province; it is the western gateway to the Canadian Shield and consequently all the lakes and forests that are part of it. Manitoba has many distinct First Nations' communities scattered throughout the province. Many of these aboriginal communities have been there for thousands of years and have learned to survive in harsh winters. Perhaps as a result, Manitobans are great fans of outdoor sports such as cross country, snowshoeing and sometimes snowmobiling. The omnipresence of snow during the winter has motivated locals to overcome the natural vertical limitations. Thus Manitoba has a few small ski areas. Parts of Manitoba even make Saskatchewan seem hilly!

Holiday Mountain (☎ 204-242-2172) at La Rivière has four lifts and **Mystery Mountain** (☎ 204-778-7434) 10 kilometres from Thompson has three surface lifts for 18 runs.

McCreary (☎ 204-835-2246) near Agassiz has 15 runs and four lifts. **Falcon Ski Area** (☎ 204-349-2201) has 16 runs. **Springhill Winter Park** has a few runs as does **Stony Mountain Winter Park**.

Thunderhill Ski Club (☎ 204-734-2919) at Swan River has 14 runs and the **Minnedosa Ski Valley** (☎ 204-867-3509) has seven runs.

PART 5: ONTARIO

Skiing Ontario

With nearly 11 million people, Ontario is Canada's most populous province and the nation's second largest in area. While this massive province spreads hundreds of kilometres north to south and east to west, the vast majority of the population lives in the far south in the low peninsula running between the Great Lakes. The entire rolling farmland from the Ottawa valley, along the coast of lake Ontario, and south to the US border is lower in latitude than the whole of western Canada. In fact Windsor is the same latitude as northern California. As the south of Ontario is in the middle of the continent and is surrounded by water, winters are certainly as harsh as in the rest of southern Canada and of course there is plenty of snow.

Although the topography of Ontario is diverse, the majority of the province is Canadian Shield with huge quantities of water flowing down into the Great Lakes or up into Hudson's Bay. The only area of the province which has any significant elevation is along its eastern border with Québec and even then the highest elevation attained in Ontario is less than 700m. Nonetheless, Ontarians have devised all sorts of ways to enjoy winter and their presence is always felt on the slopes of Québec and western Canada.

The western side of Ontario is closer to Winnipeg than Toronto and its inhabitants enjoy a beautiful lake environment with plenty of snow and cross-country opportunities, while the populated south is reminiscent of the British countryside.

While Ontario doesn't offer high elevations and therefore long runs, the province is full of smaller regional hills with surprisingly good lift systems – having the biggest population in Canada has its benefits! These hills are often great places to learn to ski and to maintain ability. Perhaps as a result of Ontarians' love of skiing, or perhaps just good planning by some of the resorts, many ski areas have some challenging runs. Most resorts with over 100 vertical metres can boast at least one one-kilometre run and the odd resort has slopes three times longer – poling included.

The other pleasure of skiing Ontario has to do with the snow. If mother nature doesn't supply enough, comprehensive snowmaking is usually possible because the resorts are small. Few things are as beautiful as a perfect patch of white in late fall or early spring.

Locals always have their favourite slopes, though there is lots of competition in some areas with new runs opening and others expanding and changing. The following can only be viewed as an outline to downhill availability. Cross-country fans and snowmobilers have hundreds of options throughout the province.

Snowboarding
Boarders and pipe fans will have a good time on Ontario's hills as many have built snowboard parks which make up for the low verticals. Perhaps lift and line-up fatigue is why so many people are taking up the sport. On smaller hills there is even a financial advantage to walking up a pipe instead of riding a short lift. No wonder the larger resorts put their pipes half-way up the mountain!

Getting around Ontario

For someone driving along the Trans-Canada through western Ontario for the first time there has to be a sense of being on an endless road to nowhere. However the sentiment is almost opposite when driving along the southern corridor from Ottawa to the American border. Highway #401 running south west from Toronto is Canada's busiest and can be absolutely terrifying during winter.

The driving conditions in eastern Canada are surprisingly different from the west. Where BC has mountain passes, the east can have freezing rain and the snow is both heavier and wetter. Roads are salted as well as gravelled and the temperatures are warmer though the humidity cuts through clothing just as easily as the -20°C temperature does in Alberta.

Flying in Ontario is easy and comprehensive. Ottawa is the most likely port of arrival for people flying in to ski, although that's only because it is the closest major city to the slopes of Québec!

North-western Ontario

The far west of Ontario is a better spot for ice fishing than downhill skiing, although there is a small hill near **Atikokan** (☎ 807-597-6624), and one further north near **Goldpines** (☎ 807-222-3716). **Kenora** also has a bump and some beautiful cross-country skiing.

The city of **Thunder Bay** nestled along the north-west shore of Lake Superior has several downhill and cross-country areas for those who need a break from driving. **Loch Lomond Ski Area** (☎ 807-475-5250) has a quad and night skiing and **Candy Mountain Resorts Ltd** (☎ 807-475-5633) has interchangeable lift passes with Loch Lomond. Of course Thunder Bay is also home to the **Big Thunder Training Centre** where, in conjunction with Calgary, crazy Canadian fliers have prepared for Olympic ski jumping and luge. There is however some question as to whether the facility will remain open. Also along the north coast **Marathon** has a small ski area.

North and central Ontario

The far north is for snowmobiles, canoes and aeroplanes but not cars. There are a few cross-country and alpine spots along the #11. South and east from **Timmins** the number of bumps with lifts begin to multiply. Eleven kilometres north of **Moonbeam** there is a tiny hill in René Brunelle Provincial Park.

Timmins (☎ 705-268-9057) has a hill nearby with two quads. There are several small resorts near the Québec border around Kirkland and Latchford. Matawa has skiing close to the town and **North Bay** has the **Laurentian Ski Club** (☎ 705-474-9950 or ☎ 1-800-663-2754).

There are several lifts around the town of **Sault Ste Marie**. **Searchmont Resort** (☎ 705-781-2340), 19 kilometres from Moonbeam drops 210m and has three chairs. **Sudbury** also has skiing – the **Capreol Ski Club** (☎ 705-858-1432) has downhill and cross-country just north of town.

Elliot Lake, the wonderful, revamped retirement community, has **Mount Dufour Ski Area** (☎ 705-848-6655).

❏ **TOURIST INFORMATION**
Travel Ontario
Queen's Park
Toronto
Ontario M7A 2E5
☎ 1-800-668-2746 or ☎ 1-800-268-3736 (French)

Eastern and southern Ontario

Pembroke has a small hill and Pakenham has 90 vertical metres. There are a couple of small hills in the Barry's Bay area near **Algonquin Provincial Park**.

The north shore of **Lake Ontario** has a few bumps and lots of cross country, even **Toronto** itself has a bit of skiing with 40 metres vertical. Less than an hour from Toronto, **Hockley Valley Resort** (☎ 519-942-0754) has a quad and 100m vertical.

The **Barrie** area north of Toronto is the closest area to the city with alpine and cross-country skiing. **Collingwood** is home to Ontario's largest resort and **Huntsville** has skiing close by at **Hidden Valley** (☎ 705-789-1773).

Blue Mountain Resorts (☎ 705-445-0231 or ☎ 416-869-3799 in Toronto) is Ontario's largest ski area. Thirteen kilometres west of Collingwood, Blue Mountain has 216 vertical metres (rather a lot for Ontario!) and 15 lifts servicing the area. This includes a quad, three triples and eight double chairs. Blue Mountain also has all the trimmings of a resort with swimming, hiking and the requisite massages.

Perhaps more stunning is **Mount St Louis Moonstone** (☎ 705-835-2112 or ☎ 416-368-6900 in Toronto) on highway #400, 35 kilometres from Barrie. This conglomerate area has 13 lifts to tackle the 150m of vertical as well as two chalets.

The **London Ski Club** (☎ 519-657-8295) uses a quad to mount its 39 metres.

And finally the transformation is complete! Canada's first **Snowboard Only** area, **The Snowboard Ranch** (☎ 705-277-9211 or ☎ 1-800-565-9146), 30 kilometres from Peterborough, has 10 runs, four lifts and 100% snowmaking!

Many other communities have small local hills which may not show on maps.

PART 6: QUEBEC

Skiing Québec

As the heart and soul of Francophone North America and Canada's second largest province, Québec offers a cultural singularity not necessarily found in Canada's younger provinces. As the old adage cries out 'Mon pays c'est l'hiver' (my country *is* winter), Québecois have endured five centuries of northern life and have developed a relationship with their climate that is perhaps unique in Canada.

The two principal metropolitan areas are Québec City, arguably Canada's most historic and architecturally beautiful city, and of course Montréal, formerly Canada's largest city. In area, Québec is the largest province in Canada, although the north remains the somewhat inaccessible domain of the Cree and their great competitor, Hydro Québec. This leaves the vast majority of people straddling the St Lawrence from the Atlantic to Ontario. The land of Québec certainly does not offer the wild diversity of BC, but the province does undulate significantly more than other provinces of eastern Canada. Generally Québec's population is much more involved in winter than summer sports.

A vacation in Québec also exposes the visitor to the benefit of its culture. While the feel of the province is more Canadian than European, Québec demonstrates the best of both worlds, particularly in song and food. At the lower end of the food chain one can race towards cardiac arrest with Québec's own *poutine*, a mix of fries, cheese curds and gravy – enough to fortify even the most weary skier!

Although Québec cannot boast the same towering mountains as does western Canada, its numerous ski destinations deserve more than a cursory acknowledgement. Indeed Québec has managed to develop resorts with an appeal far beyond its boundaries. While skiers may not want to give up their reservations at Whistler, or fly from Calgary to Québec for a ski vacation, the resorts of Québec do provide ample variety and après ski flair to make a trip from eastern North America worthwhile.

Snow conditions are very different from the west and the powder is not always a blessing as the dampness can make it incredibly heavy. When there isn't a huge pile of sticky snow, or after the groomer passes by, the snow tends to remain granular and crusty. The slopes seem built more for speed than comfort and well-sharpened edges are absolutely imperative. However, rain has been known to fall during the winter, which obviously softens up the hills. Generally, the cold winters and wide pre-planned runs permit the infrequent skier to enjoy much of a mountain. While experts usually fall in love with powder, many skiers appreciate the well-treated snow of the east because it is easy to turn on.

❏ **Free-style skiing**
As free-style skiing has gained Olympic acclaim over the past decade, Canada has performed strongly in international competition. Within Canada, Québec produces the greatest number of competitors with Jean-Luc Brassard, the 1994 Olympic Champion being the best known. After watching the extreme physical stress of the mogul event one quickly understands why free-style is a sport for young knees.

Snowboarding is a little less popular in the east of Canada, but the sport is growing quickly. The half-pipe has been introduced and Mont-Sainte-Anne near Québec City was the first to use a pipe machine. If the tradition of free-style skiing is any indication, the sport of snowboarding can expect to enjoy further growth in Québec.

The resorts of Québec have generally done an exceptional job building a variety of runs from beginner to expert and most skiers will be able to find something to please them. As a result of the lack of truly rugged terrain the scale of difficulty can err to the easier end, although there are certain runs in Québec which are as challenging as anywhere in Canada.

Of course cross-country skiing is almost second nature to many Québecois and the number of tracks is incredible. For those who find it all a bit too tiring, snowmobiling is also a very popular winter pastime.

As so many skiers in Québec are from out of province, language is rarely a problem and prices are generally good – particularly for the many Americans who make the trip up.

Climate

Québec's winter weather can vary incredibly and while the general temperatures are higher than in western Canada, the frigid winter humidity can more than make up for the difference. Of course the humidity also generates generous snowfalls which have an impressive ability to remain on the ground for months. Québec's snow is certainly nothing like the light powder atop the Rockies, but is reminiscent of the heavy wet snow of Vancouver Island. Clearing one's driveway is a formidable task.

Extremely cold spells do occur, but the cities are well-equipped. Montréal has all sorts of underground facilities so the real problem is on the roads – particularly with the freezing rain that can paralyse central Canada. Overall Québec is not oppressively cold and winter can often be soft and beautiful.

Getting around Québec

Driving can sometimes be an adventure in 'La Belle' province as many roads display the ravages of heavy snowfalls. Following the signs to Mont Tremblant from Montréal's Dorval airport, you may wonder if the highways are maintained at all. Fortunately the major routes generally have two or three lanes in either direction and drivers are much calmer once you are out of Montréal.

Orleans Coach Company (☎ 1-800-419-8735) has services through much of the province and offers good discounts for students.

Most of the province is easily accessible for eastern Canadians, and Americans from New England have an interesting and affordable destination within a day's drive. Flying is another option, with an airport in Québec City and two major airports around Montréal.

Perhaps the most difficult aspect of travelling in Québec, aside from the expected ice, is the illegality of non-French signs. One need not worry too much however as routes are very well marked with non-offensive symbols instead of words. The staff in resort areas generally speak some English and Québecois are a friendly and open group. Of course it is always worth trying a few words of French, as it is a courtesy Québecois deserve. Canada is a bilingual nation with its roots going back further in French than English.

It is illegal to turn right on a red light in Québec, and highways, as elsewhere in Canada are well patrolled.

Montréal

While no longer Canada's largest municipality, Montréal retains the cosmopolitan feel which has made it a world-class city. With its mix of western and southern Europeans along with its Jewish community and the more recent Afro-Caribbean immigration one can never go hungry or feel bored. The city does perhaps seem a little rundown but its tangible sense of history and North American grandeur are ever-present. After spending a few days strolling the streets of wintry Montréal it quickly becomes apparent how this city was the impetus for the development of the thousands of ski runs both north and south.

While this island city has long been a centre for commerce, its early entrepreneurs created the Canadian economy by opening the country's resources to international trade. The relationship Québec maintains with its environment is strong, although the snowmobiles and lumber trucks challenge that purity.

The old and new buildings sit next to each other comfortably in Montréal and wealthy families have traditionally combined their resources to develop the countless winter and summer resorts that encircle the city. The sporting regions of Québec are much less exclusive these days but they still retain that vibrant relaxed sophistication that is so much a part of Québec.

The Laurentians
(Laurentides)

Stretching north from the St Lawrence and the island of Montréal, the Laurentians are the mountains of the east. While the mountains are no challenge to the Western Cordillera, they are also not in competition. Settlement of Québec's mountain region is almost as old as Montréal itself and the variety of villages and resorts is fabulous. Though the mountains of Québec do not tower above their valleys, there still remains a unique beauty. The best way to visit the Laurentians and the whole of Québec is to come during autumn to enjoy the dramatic colours and then to stay for the snow to fall. Part of the region's appeal is its proximity to Montréal and the Ottawa/Hull area.

Skiing is the region's winter drawcard with enough visitors to attract Intrawest – the same gang that brought you Whistler and Panorama. Their masterpiece in the Laurentians is Mont Tremblant – eastern Canada's largest ski resort. While Tremblant is the largest, it is certainly not the only destination to choose from. Mont Blanc has the second highest elevation in the province and Saint Sauveur still attracts Montréal's upper classes.

Getting around the Laurentians
Should you fly to Mirabel in the north of Montréal you are literally on the region's doorstep and Dorval, Montréal's main airport, also offers easy access. Driving north is easy along the #15 super highway, or the more scenic #117. Almost everywhere you want to go is well marked.

There are many other routes that wind up from Ontario; skiers from Ottawa and Hull can be on the slopes within an hour.

MONT TREMBLANT

Tremblant, the flagship of Québec's ski industry, has that 'oh so Intrawest' feel but fortunately with undertones of Québec in both appearance and feel. The resort itself is not completely new as the old Tremblant village still exists on the edge of the provincial park. The resort consists of two ski areas, Tremblant, and the much smaller and perhaps more exclusive **Gray Rocks** (☎ 819-425-2771 or ☎ 1-800-567-6767). One of Québec's oldest ski areas, Gray Rocks still has a feel of privacy about its traditional lodge and the 22 runs are serviced by four lifts. As a result of Tremblant's development, or perhaps the economic downturn in Québec, Grey Rocks has some very affordable packages starting from under $100 inclusive.

As major resorts go Tremblant is not terribly expensive, though it may not be too many years before it grows as large as Whistler if the constant construction is any indication. It would seem possible the ski area itself could also expand sometime in the future. For the moment Tremblant is just the right size with all the amenities of a first-class, year-round resort within walking, or skiing, distance.

The developers of Tremblant have done a very good job in building the runs and the lift system is excellent. The mountain is just the right size to allow a couple of high-speed quads to go from bottom to top within a reasonable amount of time. Runs are generally quite long and are in fact some of the longest in eastern Canada.

Perhaps the biggest challenge to a good day skiing is the fog which is known to hang around the hill. However a blue sky is also very common and with the cover down on the Express Tremblant quad the whole mountain can be skied in the coldest of weather.

Although much of the hill is posted with Black Diamonds it is really an intermediate terrain with extensive grooming. Vertige and Zig Zag provide a bit of steep, bumpy fun and the trees off the Edge quad are worth a visit just after fresh snowfalls.

The north side which doubles as the back is home to Expo, perhaps the most popular area for mogul fans – it's really not too tough. The choice for beginners is easy with Nansen being six kilometres long and just steep enough not to pole.

Although the lift system is excellent and the staff efficient, the reality of a mountain this size is the lines at the bottom, and although the wait is never long the majority of skiers funnel down through just a few places. This nuisance is of course a problem on all mountains not high enough for two lift levels. The solution? Win Lotto Québec, quit work and only ski mid-week!

Snowboarding

Mais oui, Tremblant is geared as much to boards as skis and there is something about that Québecois flair that attracts more and more youths to boarding. An unscientific analysis might conclude there are slightly fewer boards than on the hills of the west, though any difference would be negligible.

There is a good park with a half-pipe on the south side – to find it just listen for the music! Fast boarding and slalom are also very popular.

Cross country

In classic Québec style, Tremblant and the surrounding area offer innumerable trails that are marked and groomed. Experienced cross-country fans can head out from the

---

❑ **Québec Tax**
If you are not Canadian, keep your receipts! On some items, ie anything you didn't consume in the province, you may be entitled to a tax refund on departure. This holds true throughout the country with regard to the federal GST, but only in Québec, Ontario and Manitoba for the provincial version (PST).

Mont Tremblant – South side

top of the mountain or from the many routes at the base. Starting from the **Centre d'accueil de Sainte-Donat** (☎ 819-688-2281) you can ski in Park du Mont-Tremblant; trail tickets cost $6.

Lessons and rentals

In terms of learning how to ski or snowboard, Tremblant is fully equipped and to drive the point home just read the advertising all over the mountain. A 90-minute skiing or boarding lesson with an instructor and only three people costs $35 in the morning and $27 after lunch! Fourteen hours of instruction over a week costs $165. Tremblant also has a program exclusively for women – between January and March ladies can ski or board with a lesson and lunch for $59. The price includes free day care for the first

Mont Tremblant – North side

child and half price for additional children. Of course private lessons are available as well as intermediate and advanced instruction. Telemark lessons can be had for $29 per hour. Equipment can be rented right at the base for $20 (and up) per day and all this can be done in English as well as French!

Tremblant has a good program for people with reduced mobility. There are also the requisite day care and ski programs for the kids.

Lift tickets
Regular adult lift tickets cost a hefty $49 per day; reduced rates are still quite high. All sorts of packages exist in conjunction with hotels and multi-day tickets. A Max card ($45 adult or $35 youth/student) entitles you to get your first lift ticket free; you also

save $10 on a lift ticket for Mondays to Thursdays, $7 for a ticket on Fridays and Sundays and $2 on Saturdays and holidays. You can ski free on your sixth visit so the card is particularly worthwhile if you buy it early in the season.

Getting there and around

This is the easy part. Tremblant is 120 kilometres north of Montréal and can be easily reached within 1 1/2 hours. Drive north along #15 until it merges with the #117 then follow the signs from Ste Jovite. A shuttle (☎ 1-888-868-7702) can be arranged from either of the Montréal airports from $33; call at least two days ahead.

Ottawa/Hull is about two hours further on, whereas Toronto is at least seven hours. Québec city is 3 1/2 hours away and has good skiing much closer by.

Once at Tremblant, getting around is easy. The Intrawest resort is a pedestrian only resort, but there is a shuttle that tours the greater area. You may choose to stay in one of the smaller guest houses or hotels around the village in which case you'll have to drive or use the shuttle. There is all sorts of well-managed parking available; the park nearest the slopes – for those who really hate walking – charges $9.

Accommodation

If you're not 100% sure about taking a trip to Tremblant a deciding factor could be that first-class shelter here will not break the bank and once out of the resort itself the range of options increases considerably. All the accommodation available on the hill is of a high standard. If you haven't pre-booked stop in at one of the tourist information centres (☎ 819-425-8681) for a list of options.

Budget skiers may like to try Tremblant International Youth Hostel (☎ 819-425-6008); the hostel has 84 beds and prices start at under $16 – reservations are essential. Everyone else may want to start by getting an information package from Central Reservations (☎ 1-800-567-6760). All-inclusive fly-and-ski packages from Toronto and many of the major US cities start from around US$500 for five days.

Canadian Pacific has come up trumps with the *Château Mont Tremblant* (☎ 819-681-7000 or ☎ 1-800-441-1414). Mid season two people can stay two nights and ski two days for around $400; expect to pay a lot more during holiday periods. Five-night ski weeks in regular season are slightly over $500 per person.

Marriott's comfortable *Residence Inn* (☎ 1-888-272-4000) is perfectly located and has comparable prices. The *Intrawest Resort Club* is slightly less expensive and

---

❏ MONT TREMBLANT
Base elevation: 265m (870ft)
Summit: 915m (3,001ft)
Vertical: 650m (2,131ft)
Lifts: 6 quads (1 covered), 2 triples and 4 surface
77 runs: 15 beginner, 24 intermediate and 38 advanced
Average snowfall: 370cm (145in), snow falls from November to May, often in several large dumps.
(There are enough snow guns to cover almost the entire hill.)

Contacts
Information and reservations: ☎ 819-681-2000 or ☎ 1-800-461-8711
Central Reservations: ☎ 1-800-567-6760
Accommodation information: ☎ 819-425-8681
Snow phone: ☎ Montréal 514-333-8936; Toronto ☎ 905-889-7346; Ottawa ☎ 613-237-1186
Gray Rocks: ☎ 819-425-2771 or ☎ 1-800-567-6767
Home page: www.tremblant.ca

well equipped (☎ 1-800-799-3258 ext 702). *Sunstar Resorts* (☎ 1-800-754-8736) has roomy condos which can be fair value if eight people get together. Two-day, two-night deals in low season can be under $140 per person.

Les Suites (1-800-461-8711) has hundreds of rooms throughout the resort – Prices start from $75 per person. However at *Place St-Bernard* which is in the heart of the resort and *Le Kandahar,* their fabulous new facility, expect to pay about $140 per person.

Après ski
The number of bars – eleven including one for teens only – should offer some indication of the nightlife available. Tremblant also has a great selection of restaurants spread throughout the resort – even the on-hill food is quite good but it is overpriced.

Most of the hotels have up-scale restaurants with first-class chefs. The village restaurants have a faint resemblance to the bistros in Québec City; overall prices are reasonable. *La Diable* brews its own beer and often has live music. *Café-Bistro Ryan* has reasonable prices for breakfast and lunch. *Pizzateria* is good and well priced.

More pricey but highly recommended is *Aux Truffes* (☎ 819-681-4544), open from 6pm to 10pm; it is worth making a reservation. The *Bullseye Bar & Grill* (☎ 819-681-2855) has big steaks and seafood. Reservations are also recommended.

Please note that these are but a few of the culinary options and during high season everywhere is crowded. Of course the many condos have their own facilities and stocking up is just a short drive away.

Other
As Tremblant has entered the realm of major resorts there is certainly a wide variety of ski-less activities one can pursue. Snowshoeing, horseback riding and dogsledding are all popular. As is true throughout Québec, snowmobiles are always around and when the outdoor activities are all said and done, head for **La Source Aquatic Park** to unwind. This wonderfully relaxing environment is right beside the Marriott hotel; an adult day pass costs $16.

MONT BLANC
Ten kilometres before St-Jovite along route #117 is Mont Blanc, with the second highest vertical in the region at 300m (nearly 1,000ft). Mont Blanc's 77 runs, on two mountains, are well constructed with a fairly even distribution for all levels. The mountain is serviced by one quad, two triples, a double and four surface lifts, so for a terrain this size, lift lines are not a great worry. Lifts operate between 8.30am and 4pm.

As many of these moderately-sized resorts have done, Mont Blanc has transformed itself into a good place at which to learn to ski with an excellent variety of packages available, starting from $35 inclusive (rental, lesson and lift ticket; three person minimum). Bumps are left to form on several runs and one area of the hill is only for intermediate skiers or better. Beginners as well as skiers with a little more experience can enjoy the majority of the mountain.

During the week, lift tickets are an affordable $20 ($18 for seniors (60-69) and youth (13-20), $15 for juniors (6-12). Seniors over 70 and children aged 5 and under ski free. At weekends and holidays the price climbs to $30 ($25 for seniors and youth and $19 for juniors). Boarders will be happy with the half-pipe and there is a loop for cross-country fans.

❑ **MONT BLANC**
Information and reservations: ☎ 819-688-2444 or ☎ 1-800-567-6715
Home page: www.ski-mont-blanc.com

Mont Blanc

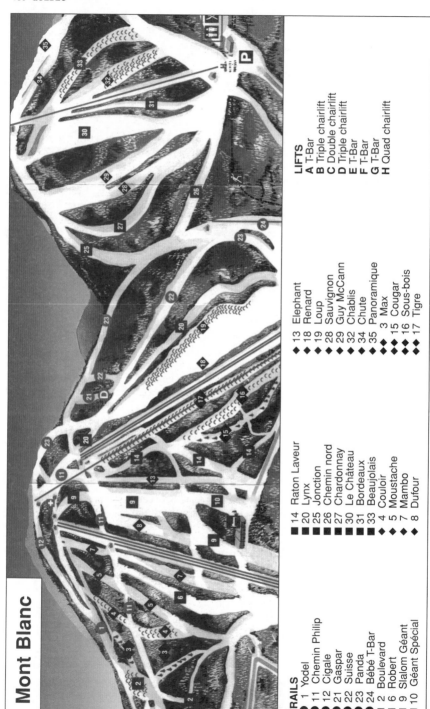

TRAILS

● 1 Yodel
● 11 Chemin Philip
● 12 Cigale
● 21 Gaspar
● 22 Suisse
● 23 Panda
● 24 Bébé T-Bar
■ 2 Boulevard
■ 6 Robert
■ 9 Slalom Géant
■ 10 Géant Spécial

■ 14 Raton Laveur
■ 20 Lynx
■ 25 Jonction
■ 26 Chemin nord
■ 27 Chardonnay
■ 30 Le Château
■ 31 Bordeaux
■ 33 Beaujolais
◆ 4 Couloir
◆ 5 Moustache
◆ 7 Mambo
◆ 8 Dufour

◆ 13 Elephant
◆ 18 Renard
◆ 19 Loup
◆ 28 Sauvignon
◆ 29 Guy McCann
◆ 32 Chablis
◆ 34 Chute
◆ 35 Panoramique
◆ 3 Max
◆ 15 Cougar
◆ 16 Sous-bois
◆ 17 Tigre

LIFTS
A T-Bar
B Triple chairlift
C Double chairlift
D Triple chairlift
E T-Bar
F T-Bar
G T-Bar
H Quad chairlift

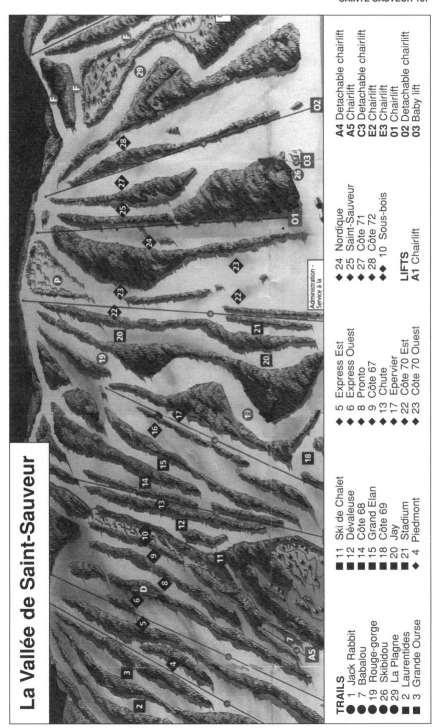

La Vallée de Saint-Sauveur

TRAILS

- ● 1 Jack Rabbit
- ● 7 Babalou
- ● 19 Rouge-gorge
- ● 26 Skibidou
- ● 29 Grande Ourse
- ■ 2 Laurentides
- ■ 3 Grande Ourse

- ■ 11 Ski de Chalet
- ■ 12 Dévaleuse
- ■ 14 Côte 68
- ■ 15 Grand Elan
- ■ 18 Côte 69
- ■ 20 Jay
- ■ 21 Stadium
- ◆ 4 Piedmont

- ◆ 5 Express Est
- ◆ 6 Express Ouest
- ◆ 8 Pronto
- ◆ 9 Côte 67
- ◆ 17 Chute
- ◆ 17 Epervier
- ◆ 22 Côte 70 Est
- ◆ 23 Côte 70 Ouest

- ◆ 24 Nordique
- ◆ 25 Saint-Sauveur
- ◆ 27 Côte 71
- ◆ 28 Côte 72
- ◆ 10 Sous-bois

LIFTS

- A1 Chairlift
- A4 Detachable chairlift
- A5 Chairlift
- C3 Detachable chairlift
- E2 Chairlift
- E3 Chairlift
- O1 Chairlift
- O2 Detachable chairlift
- O3 Baby lift

Administration - Service à la

❏ **LA VALLEE DE SAINT-SAUVEUR**
Information and reservations ☎ 514-227-4671 or ☎ 1-800-363-2426
Home page: www.montsaintsauveur.com

LA VALLEE DE SAINT–SAUVEUR

Just 60 kilometres from Montréal, the skiing around Saint-Sauveur is the closest to the city and offers a genuine choice of descents. The five resorts in the valley share marketing and, a real bonus to skiers, they accept each other's lift tickets. Each of the resorts has around 200 vertical metres (650ft) which keeps them out of the major resort league, but with 95 runs serviced by 35 lifts the valley remains popular with Montréalers. Saint-Sauveur is a great place to not ski too hard while showing off your new equipment, clothing and car! The accommodation is beautiful and often traditional with several attractive manors reminiscent of Montréal's colonial past.

The five ski areas are Mont Saint-Sauveur, Mont Avila, Morin Heights, Mont Gabriel and Mont Olympia with Saint-Sauveur/Avila being the largest. The two hills are in essence one and have a total of 30 runs, almost all of which utilise the entire vertical. Condos run up the hill at several places and the base of Saint-Sauveur has all the amenities such as day care and ski schools.

Off to the side of Mont Avila is a Tube park. Almost the entire ski area is well groomed with the odd spot for a bit of tree skiing. There are two snowboard parks and a half-pipe on Mont Avila off the L'Express chair.

Snowmaking is comprehensive throughout the valley and access along the #15 highway is easy. Speed limits throughout the resort are strictly enforced.

OTHER LAURENTIANS

Further up the Laurentians from Saint-Sauveur are the village areas of Val-David and Val-Morin. These are beautiful winter spots enhanced by fantastic snow carvings and winter festivals. The guest houses are popular, particularly with cross-country skiers who come to enjoy the route between Val-David and Saint-Jerome which follows the former railroad line. The route is known as **Le Parc lineaire Le P'tit Train du Nord**. A guide service (☎ 514-436-8532) is available.

Downhill skiers can easily stay in the Val David/Val Morin area and ski the major resorts, but closer by are the resorts of **Belle Neige** (14 runs, ☎ 819-322-3311), **Vallée-Bleue** (16 runs, ☎ 819-322-3427) and **Mont-Alta** (22 runs, ☎ 819-322-3206).

Close to Sainte-Adèle is **Chantecler** (☎ 514-229-2476) with a 200m vertical and 22 runs. Lift tickets for children (0-5) and seniors (70+) cost $5 a day and also for night skiing; those aged 6-12 or 55-69 pay $12 Monday to Friday, $15 on weekends/holidays and $10 for night skiing; and if you're between 13 and 54, you pay $15 Monday to Friday, $22 on weekends/holidays and $10 for night skiing (this rises to $15 on Fridays, Saturdays and holidays).

Lifts start operating at 9am during the week and from 8.30am on Saturdays and Sundays. Some close between 4 and 5.30pm but those which are used for night skiing stay open till 10pm.

Québec City region

While there are all sorts of great reasons for skiing the resorts around Québec's capital, perhaps the single most enticing is the opportunity to visit the city itself. Old Québec (Vieux Québec) remains the heart of French Canada. The city is the site of the Plains of Abraham where, in 1759, British troops scaled cliffs from the St Lawrence to defeat the royal French army and lay claim to almost all of North America.

After that violent encounter Québec was attacked by the Americans but the local French sided with the British eventually and participated in the creation of Canada. Old Québec is now North America's only walled city and its compelling, old world architecture is so outstanding that the city has been registered as a World Heritage site by the United Nations.

Québec is a pleasure to visit during any season, but if there was any major Canadian city that is perhaps more attractive during winter than summer it would have to be Québec. Nestled at a narrowing point of the St Lawrence's north shore, the city overlooks the frozen river. The culmination of winter fun in Québec comes during mid-February when the winter festival brings the entire region to life with ice sculptures, entertainers and, of course, parties. This is the most lively regular winter event in Canada and it attracts thousands of visitors annually.

Skiers from elsewhere in North America looking for a touch of old world charm do not need to make the trek across the Atlantic. A similar ambience can be found in Québec for a fraction of the cost and with all the amenities of North America. After a good day on the many surrounding slopes, Old Québec is a great place to wander, stopping every now and then at the many cafés and pubs. The food is delicious and the service good and often bilingual. This noted, it is always polite to ask whether someone speaks English and to offer at least a customary *merci* in lieu of thank you.

The city's French atmosphere is palpable with artists selling their wares on the street and scarves worn just so. Québec nonetheless rests very firmly in the Great White North, so you can always take your cross-country skis out to the Plains of Abraham, and drink beer from the bottle!

Getting there and around

Québec is on the north side of the St Lawrence River (*Fleuve Saint-Laurent*), about three hours east of Montréal. Good highways run along both sides of the river, and roads are generally better in this part of the province. If you're arriving from the river's south side, which is most likely, follow the signs to the Pierre-LaPorte Bridge (*Pont Pierre-LaPorte*). Once on the north side just follow the signs to Vieux Québec. The newer part of the city is easy to drive in. Districts have different names as Québec is a conglomeration of separately administered cities.

Once you reach Québec's outskirts follow the signs to the very helpful Greater Québec Area Tourism and Convention Bureau; you will be given a good map and

---

❏ **TOURIST INFORMATION**
Greater Québec Area Tourism and Convention Bureau
399, rue Saint- Joseph Est
Québec
G1K 8E2
☎ 418-522-3511   Home page www.quebec-region.cuq.qc.ca

information free of charge. Québec's airport is close to town, although many international flights will go through Montréal first.

Essentially all roads lead to the old city, and the beautiful walls are impossible to miss. Cars are permitted to drive in Old Québec, however parking on the street is mostly restricted to residents, so it is worth finding one of the underground lots and just walk. Everything is close and the narrow streets are much more pleasant on foot.

Of course the city as a whole is one of Canada's largest and therefore it has all of the amenities and annoyances with public transportation, shopping malls and traffic associated with a city, though stress levels here are generally much lower than in Montréal.

Getting around the Québec region is easy and, as elsewhere in Québec, tourist sites are well marked. If you don't have a car, or do not want to drive, there is a winter shuttle (☎ 418-525-5191) that runs from different hotels to many areas of the region including three ski resorts.

Accommodation
Many of Québec's ski areas have good on-site hotels and condos that are also within an easy drive of the city, though for the first-time visitor a stay in Québec itself can be enchanting.

Obviously as a major city and a capital, Québec is overflowing with accommodation options for almost all budgets. For tourists who want to stay in the centre of Old Québec, the most affordable and friendly choice is one of the many guest houses. Most have doubles for well under $100. Pick up an accommodation guide at the Tourism and Convention Bureau or call for one in advance. Another budget option is *Hostelling International* (☎ 418-694-0755) which has a great hostel inside the walls with dorm beds for $17.

The crème de la crème of Québec's hotels and indeed one of Canada's most beautiful and famous, is the dominating *Château Frontenac (*☎ 418-692-3861 or Canadian Pacific Reservations ☎ 1-800-441-1414) Standing gracefully above the old city, the Château is another masterpiece in Canadian Pacific's chain of first-class hotels across the country. If you have never visited Québec, but have seen photos, they likely include the Château. Luxury is not cheap, but with doubles from $200 in low season, a night in a castle is not out of reach.

Skiing Québec City
The skiing around Québec City is close and generally excellent. Annual snowfalls are around 400cm and the resorts have good grooming. The largest resort is Mont Sainte Anne – it is also perhaps Québec's best with its views of the city and the St Lawrence. Several other destinations can be reached within an hour.

The south shore of the river is very flat, whereas the north side rises up into the eastern Laurentians, with the mountains rolling north to Labrador. The snow is often quite crusty, particularly on the resorts along the river, and the powder can be so heavy that good grooming is appreciated. There are several resorts directly north of the city, all within twenty minutes.

The diversity of skiing around Québec makes the region a worthwhile destination for most skiers, and cross-country fans are in their element. So are snowmobilers!

LE RELAIS
The closest ski area to the city, Le Relais is a mere 15 minutes due north along route #73N. Should Québec ever host the Winter Olympics the ski aerials will likely be held here. Le Relais has over 15 runs with an emphasis on intermediate and advanced terrain. The snowfall is generally quite low, however 100% snowmaking guarantees a full season.

Le Relais

TRAILS

● 1 La Familiale
● 1B Le Petit Sentier
● 4 La Pente-Ecole
● 15 Charlesbourg
● 15a La Pente Douce
■ 1A Le premier Défi
■ 2 La Laurentide
■ 3C La Chrono
■ 7 Gaby Pleau
■ 8B La Promenade
■ 8C La Traverse
■ 10 La Bohème
◆ 2A La Balade
◆ 3 Laurent Bernier
◆ 3A La Banane
◆ 3B La Qui-sait-tout
◆ 3C La Chrono
◆ 5 Conrad DeLisle
◆ 8 Docteur Pouliot
◆ 8A Lac-Beauport
◆ 9 Guy A Pacquet

◆ 10A L'Etonnante
◆ 11 Jean-Claude Tremblay
◆ 12 Suzanne Proteau-Blais
◆◆ 13 La Fougerole
◆◆ 14 La Vertigineuse

LIFTS

A Tire-fesses
B T-Bar
C Quad chairlift
D Rapid T-Bar
E Tire-fesses
F Detachable quad chairlift

OTHERS

G Ski patrol
H Centre de chronometrage
I Tickets
J First Aid
K Le Refuge
L Chronometre automatique

The resort has a good lift system with two quads – one high speed – and four other surface lifts. Lifts operate between 9am and 10pm, Monday to Thursday (to 10.30pm on Fridays); and from 8.30am on Saturday (to 10.30pm) and Sunday (to 10pm). However, when there is no night skiing they stop at 5pm. The area has a 224m vertical. There is a chalet at the base with a cafeteria. For information and reservations phone ☎ 418-849-1851 and for the ski school phone ☎ 418-849-3073.

A short way further up the road is the slightly smaller **Mont-Saint-Castin** in the process of being rebuilt.

Close to the Valcartier military base is the **Centre Recreo Sportif Castor** (☎ 418-848-2415) with 14 runs.

STONEHAM

Just 20 minutes north of Québec, Stoneham is the second largest resort in the region and it boasts the most comprehensive night-skiing terrain in Canada. The village area is growing and Stoneham is becoming a fairly major and lively winter resort. In conjunction with its accessibility to Québec, the area has a myriad of affordable ways to enjoy a day's skiing.

Stoneham's circular layout resembles many of the bowls of western Canada, but is in the trees below the tree line. Most of the skiing takes place on three fairly distinct mountains so the crowds are able to spread out and the lift system is comprehensive. Most of the runs are fairly wide and the blacks are designated as such due to their steepness rather than the rough terrain. Beginners who are beyond the basic lifts might want to climb the middle mountain and ski run #19, or take double chair D to ski the three kilometre long run #6. Ski tubing is also a popular endeavour.

Snowboarding
There are a few runs not open to boards, but there are several areas for playing around. Boards are quite common and the grooming means the snow is kept in fairly good condition for making turns.

Cross country
There are quite a few centres in the area and several routes at the base of the resort.

Lessons and rentals
The ski school here offers a wide range of lessons and courses; it is popular with school groups, particularly as it is so close to Québec City. Private lessons are affordable, starting from $27 per hour – prices decrease with more people. Beginner packages start from $30 for a lift ticket, lesson and rental. There are numerous kids' programs and a day-care scheme. Snowboarding is now being taught. Rentals are $16 and

---

❏ STONEHAM
Base elevation: 212m (690ft)
Summit: 630m (2,020ft)
Vertical: 420m (1,350ft)
Lifts: 4 quads (1 detachable), 2 doubles, 4 surface
25 runs: 30% beginner, 40% intermediate, 30% advanced
Annual snowfall: N/A – 95% snowmaking
Lift operating hours: Monday to Thursday 9am-10pm, Friday 9am-10.30pm, Saturday 8.30am-10.30pm, Sunday 8.30am-9pm.

Contacts
Information and reservations: ☎ 418-848-2411 or ☎ 1-800-463-6888
Snow phone: ☎ 418-848-2415

Stoneham

boards are $30 per day – less for youths/seniors. Snowboard boots cost $5 with board.

Lift tickets

	Adult	Student/Youth	Senior
Full day	$31.59	$21.94	$18.43
Night	$15.80	$13.16	$11.41

Stoneham is one of those mountains with an awesome variety of lift rates including hourly and multi-day.

Getting there and around

Drive or take the shuttle (from downtown hotels in Québec City) straight north of Québec along route #73 and turn off at the sign for Station Touristique Stoneham. The journey takes around 20 minutes.

Accommodation and après ski

The two options for on-hill lodging are *Hotel Stoneham* and *Condominiums Stoneham*; for details of both phone ☎ 418-848-2411 or ☎ 1-800-463-6888. Doubles in the hotel can be had for under $100 in one of the 60 rooms. The fully-equipped condos have one to four rooms. A typical two-bedroom unit costs around $400, however additional nights are much less expensive.

The base lodges have a cafeteria and there is a good restaurant in the hotel. There are also a couple of lounges which have a lively atmosphere.

MONT-SAINTE-ANNE

Although perhaps somewhat shadowed by Tremblant, Sainte-Anne is arguably Québec's best ski area with a great variety of runs, good lifts, diverse terrain and fabulous views. The village area of Mont-Sainte-Anne is just outside Sainte-Anne-de-Beaupré, a town on the coast of the St Lawrence which has one of North America's most impressive cathedrals. Mont-Sainte-Anne is marketed as a four-season resort – but its real appeal is the skiing. Cross-country fans are also drawn to Sainte-Anne because it has the largest track network of any resort in Canada.

The base area has just enough restaurants and pubs to constitute a small village and the mountain is a well run, friendly resort with all necessary services. Snowfalls are relatively high and most of the mountain is well utilised. Mont-Sainte-Anne is slowly gaining acclaim and is growing in popularity internationally. Visitors are rarely

---

❏ MONT-SAINTE-ANNE
Base elevation: 175m (575ft)
Summit: 800m (2,625ft)
Vertical: 625m (2,050ft)
Lifts: 1 gondola, 3 quads, 1 covered, 1 triple, 2 doubles and 5 surface
54 runs: 24%beginner, 46% intermediate, 30% advanced
Average snowfall: 400cm (180in)
Lift operating hours: 9am-10pm Tuesday to Saturday,
8.30am-4pm Sunday and Monday.

Contacts
Information: ☎ 418-827-4561
Reservations Bureau: (☎ 418-827-5281 or ☎ 1-800-463-1568)
Snow phone: ☎ 418-827-4579 (Québec) or ☎ 514-861-6670 (Montréal);
☎ 416-597-1788 (Toronto)
Cross-country Information and reservations: ☎ 418-827-4564
Home page: www.mont-sainte-anne.com

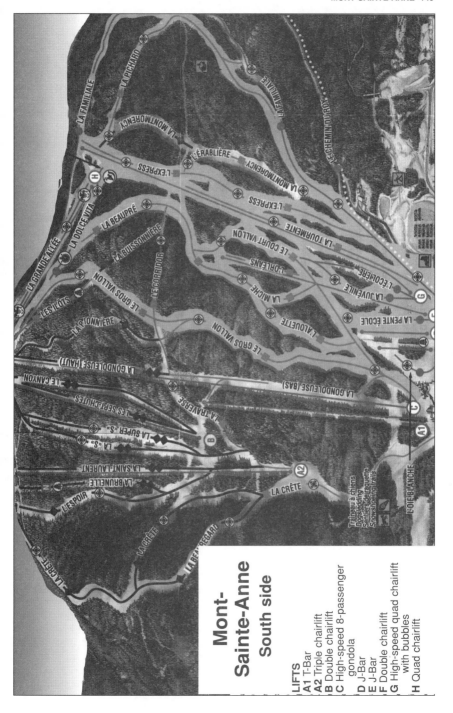

Mont-Sainte-Anne
South side

LIFTS
A1 T-Bar
A2 Triple chairlift
B Double chairlift
C High-speed 8-passenger
gondola
D J-Bar
E J-Bar
F Double chairlift
G High-speed quad chairlift
with bubbles
H Quad chairlift

disappointed, though perhaps a little colder than expected as a result of the bitter wind that blows across the south face, due to its exposure to the river.

The runs at Sainte-Anne are well designed, enjoyably long and they tend to stay at the same standard from top to bottom which is particularly pleasing to advanced skiers who tire of long green ski-outs after a good run. Lift tickets at Sainte-Anne have entered the 20th century; this means inserting cards into electronic slots before each lift. The gondola is comfortable and the ride is just long enough to justify the construction of a gondola (as opposed to a chair), though it can be a bit tiring to constantly be taking your skis on and off. The resort also boasts a covered quad which serves a large area of night and intermediate skiing. If you ride the quad, followed by the triple chair, you can descend Canada's highest night vertical!

Mont-Sainte-Anne has two sides with the village at the base of the south side. The north or backside is a more intermediate area with a little less wind and some beautiful views of the Laurentians. Intermediates will enjoy the new Sidney-Dawes run which has a less challenging tree environment.

The south is the larger face and the gondola serves as the divide between the advanced runs and the others. From the top of the gondola, experts should head for the Chalet de la Crête (open weekends only), as the area down from it is all black and is served by two chairs. The chalet has great views of Québec. The double black runs deserve their designation and if you're tired of bumps ski down La Super 'S' to enjoy a steep groomed run.

There are a couple of long sweeping beginner runs on both sides of the mountain; the rest of the runs are for intermediates. Because of the distinct area for advanced skiers, cruisers who enjoy good intermediate runs with long sweeping turns have all sorts of options without competition. The cross-country trails are open from 9am-4pm on weekdays and 8.30am-4pm on weekends.

Snowboarding
Mont-Sainte-Anne was the first resort in Québec to woo boarders, not only with a machined half-pipe but also with an excellent jumping park under the triple chair. Boarders share this area with more and more skiers who are trying out their wings. The pipe has music and is a popular spot for competitions. The rest of the mountain is open to boards and the new treed runs are great after a good snowfall.

Cross country
The 223 kilometres of classic tracks and 125km for skating mean this is the largest cross-country area in any of Canada's resorts. The track system is very well designed and well marked for difficulty. Upon arrival, just a little further on from the alpine ski area, there is a good lodge at the start of the tracks. It is possible to ski from both the south and north sides of the resort, or to drive or take the shuttle to the chalet. Warming huts have been placed throughout the area and all the routes are essentially circular, working back to the central lodge.

Tracks are fairly evenly divided between skating and classic, with a couple of long classic trails including an 18km back-country track. Many of them are wide enough for both track-set classic and skating.

A day's skiing costs $11.30 for adults, youth (14-22) $7.82, family $26.08. A five-day pass is $45.21 for an adult, $30.43 for youth (14-22) and $104.33 for a family. It is possible to spend the night in one of the huts; there are seven heated shelters of which two have accommodation for eight people. Full equipment rental goes for $13 per day.

Lessons and rentals
Needless to say, a full range of lessons are offered and Mont-Sainte-Anne is a growing destination for school groups from as far away as Europe. A two-hour group les-

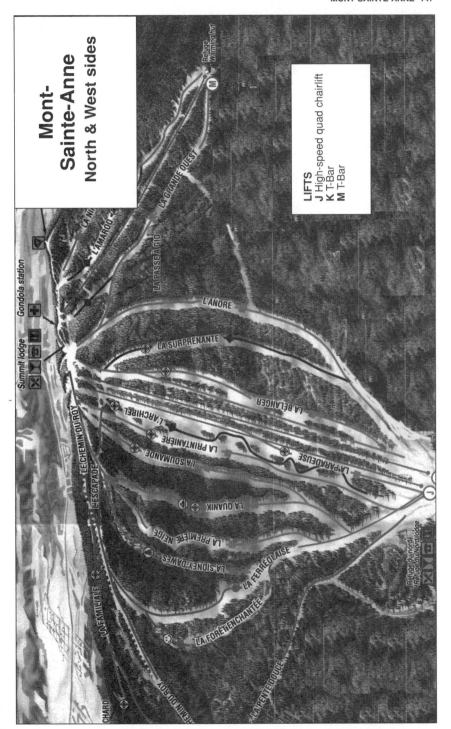

Mont-Sainte-Anne
North & West sides

LIFTS
J High-speed quad chairlift
K T-Bar
M T-Bar

Summit lodge · Gondola station

LA GRANDE OUEST

L'AMAROOK

LA PASSE À GIO

L'ANORE

LA SURPRENANTE

LA BELANGER

L'ARCHIPEL

LA PRINTANIÈRE

LA SOUMANDE

LA PARADEUSE

LE CHEMIN DU ROY

L'ESCAPADE

LA OUANIK

LA PREMIÈRE NEIGE

LA SIDNEY-DAMES

LA FERRÉOLAISE

LA FAMILIALE

LA FORÊT ENCHANTÉE

LA PENTE DOUCE

CHEMIN DU ROY

Refuge du nord
Refuge du Nord lodge

Refuge
Warming hut

son for skiers and boarders costs $32.17, the private version is $40. There are many multi-day lesson packages as well as Kinderski programs and a day-care scheme. Sainte-Anne has also jumped on the snowblades wagon and lessons are available.

Rentals are reasonable at $18.26 per day, discounted for students and multi-day. Skis can be rented for night skiing for $14.78.

Lift tickets

	Adult	Youth (14-22)	Child* (7-13)	Senior (65+)*
Full day	$37.38	$33.04	$23.47	$28.69

* Seniors aged over 70 and children aged 6 and under ski free.

The variety of ticket options is stunning, so unless you are just skiing one day don't expect to spend full price. A noon to 10pm ticket is a little less expensive and night skiing costs under $20 (from 3pm), a three-day ticket is $103.46 (adult) and a six-day ticket $162.57 (adult).

Getting there and around

Mont-Sainte-Anne is a painless 40 kilometres (25 miles) east of Québec. The resort is just a few kilometres up from the town of Ste-Anne de Beaupré; the south face can be seen from the highway. The resort is small enough not to get lost, and buses run to hotels further away from the slopes.

A shuttle is available from Québec's two bus stations (☎ 418-650-0087 (Sainte-foy) or 418-525-300 (Québec)) at reasonable prices. On Wednesday nights you can get a round trip package (bus and lift ticket) for $15.65.

Accommodation

The growing village has many condos and hotel rooms at the base, with many more on the road down to Beaupré. Life is made easy by the fact that everything can be booked through the Reservations Bureau (☎ 418-827-5281 or ☎ 1-800-463-1568).

The most central condos, **Village Touristique** (☎ 418-827-2002 or ☎ 1-800-463-7775), are part of the village; they have from one to three rooms and offer ski packages from $150 per person per night including lift tickets and one dinner. The cross-country version starts from $115 per person. These condos are ski in/out and have underground parking.

The *Chalets Mont Sainte-Anne* (condos) are also at the base of the runs and are much less expensive with ski-and-stay packages starting from $61 per person (☎ 418-827-5776 or ☎ 1-800-463-4395).

Château Mont-Sainte-Anne (☎ 418-827-5211 or ☎ 1-800-463-4467) is a little more upscale and is a four-season resort and convention centre. Inclusive packages start from $235, based on two people for two days.

There are several other large hotels in the area and with Québec City just down the road accommodation is never too difficult to find.

Après ski

The village area can be good fun at night; there are a couple of pubs and a few restaurants. Generally prices are reasonable and the food has a distinctive Québecois flair. Aside from the base area of the mountain, the *Summit Chalet* has food and drinks to enjoy while others ski into the evening. The north side has a lodge at the base of the lifts.

Other

As Mont-Sainte-Anne has fashioned itself into a full resort, many activities aside from skiing are available. The gondola runs year round and during winter you can go skating, dog-sledding, or even para-gliding from the top of the mountain – depending on the wind of course.

LIFTS
A Detachable quad chairlift
B Double chairlift
C Surface lift

OTHERS
M Cafeteria, pub, guest services
N Ski shop (rental and repair)
O Tickets and administration

LE MASSIF

Not technically in the Québec region, but within an hour of the city, Le Massif is one of Québec's best small areas and it is the proposed site for Olympic downhill competition if Quebec wins the right to host the games.

Le Massif is predominantly an advanced ski area but there are five rather narrow beginner runs and four intermediate trails. However, the big story is La '42', a narrow, bumpy double black which is almost two kilometres long. With a 630m (over 2000ft) vertical descent and no opportunity to find an easier route, this is indeed an expert run. The widest run at Le Massif is Le Sous Bois, however the liberal sprinkling of trees reserves it for experts.

Le Massif can be very cold as the base is literally metres away from the St Lawrence, and snowfalls are often wet and heavy. There are three lifts, though most of the action is off the long, high-speed chair. The lifts operate between 9am and 3pm

❑ **Carnaval de Québec**

Over the last 45 years, Québec's internationally renowned carnival has grown to be a celebration of winter that is second to none. Heralded in each year by Québec's *Bonhomme* snowman, the festival brings the city to life during the first two weeks of February. While the festival is the result of hundreds of years of Québecois culture and traditions, the concept is to get people out of their homes and on to the streets to enjoy the beauty of winter.

When enjoying Carnaval, make sure to watch the crazy locals pushing and rowing boats across the half-frozen St Lawrence – a tradition dating from early settlement on islands along the river. Just outside the city walls, looking across to the National Assembly, artists construct one of the most impressive ice sculptures in Canada.

On the boardwalk, in front of Canadian Pacific's Chateau Frontenac is an ice slide, offering a sense of early lugeing. The ride down has beautiful views of the river but can be bitterly cold if the frigid wind is blowing.

Remember to reserve a room well in advance before going to Québec for Carnaval.

during the week and between 8.30am and 3pm at the weekends – as long as the daylight is good enough. Boards are welcome. For information and reservations phone ☎ 418-632-5876.

Getting there and around

Le Massif is a good half hour further on from Mont-Sainte-Anne. Adjacent to the town of Petite-Rivière Saint-Francois, Le Massif is down a very steep road along the banks of the river. Bus and lift ticket packages (for information phone ☎ 1-800-461-0754) are available from Québec and Mont Sainte-Anne; expect to pay about $40.

Accommodation

If you're not just having a day from Sainte-Anne or Québec, Le Massif has all sorts of ski-and-stay deals organised with the many guest houses close by. Most are available for between $55 and $90 per person and the traditional village is a great place to stay for a couple of nights. Call Central Reservations for details.

The Eastern Townships
(Les Cantons-de-l'Est)

This southern area of Québec shares a long border with the United States but rests in historic opposition to Canada's republican neighbour. Perhaps this is why it is such a pleasure to see the thousands of American license plates parked at the region's excellent ski hills. Montréalers tend to grow up in different camps, either spending their vacations in the Laurentians or the Townships. It would seem that neither region has been the outright winner, but people do tend to remain faithful to their chosen destination.

The Townships came about as a result of the American War of Independence when the Loyalists (those who chose to remain loyal to the then British presence in North America) were granted territories in lower Canada. Over the years French Canadians gradually moved into the area and the region's majority is now Francophone, although the English presence is still evident. Despite Québec's unique language laws the Townships remain essentially bilingual.

Physically the Townships are beautiful and they are well established as a winter destination having some of Québec's best alpine resorts. The mountains are the northern chain of the ancient Appalachians and between the rounded hills and frozen lakes of the valleys the Eastern Townships offer a compelling environment. The area's major city is Sherbrooke with nearby Magog servicing one of the major ski areas, but the pervasive feeling is a rural one with all the resorts having a relaxed, friendly feel.

Getting there and around
The Townships are accessible from most places in the east, being less than an hour from Montréal, slightly further from Québec City, and very accessible from the states of New Hampshire, Vermont and Maine. The ski resorts also seem very popular with people from New Jersey who make the journey north by the bus load. The one significant challenge to travelling through the Townships is the truly atrocious condition of the roads which, with the exception of the #10 and #55 highways, are often icy and poorly maintained.

Driving south from Montréal the mountains gently rise up from Québec's flat farmland. The different villages are scattered along minor roads and Victorian style manors and guest houses dot the land.

Skiing the Eastern Townships
Overall, skiing in southern Québec can be great and the area's four largest ski resorts have combined forces in order to offer interchangeable tickets making a ski trip in the Townships even more attractive.

The group of four include **Bromont, Owl's Head, Orford** and **Mont Sutton**. Orford has the highest vertical, whereas Sutton is the largest area. Each resort is worth a visit and is within a manageable distance from the others. A five-day pass to all four resorts goes for $145 (youth, child (6-13) and senior (65+), $100). The pass includes night-skiing at Bromont.

Other ski areas in the Townships include **Mont Bellevue** (☎ 819-821-5872), close to Sherbrooke, with six runs and three lifts and **Montjoye** (☎ 819-821-5872) which is just outside North Hatley, south of Sherbrooke. Montjoye has 18 runs with nearly 200 vertical metres serviced by three lifts.

Mont Glen (☎ 514-243-6142) hasn't yet joined in on the multi-ticket packs, but the area does have over 300 vertical metres (1,000+ft) and 26 runs. The eight lifts here are only operated at certain times so it's worth calling ahead. Weekday lift tickets only cost $15 ($25 during weekends and holidays).

BROMONT
This is the smallest of the four resorts but it's very accessible being situated just outside the town of Bromont off the #10 highway, 45 minutes from Montréal. The resort is still expanding, but the ski area is certainly large enough for an enjoyable day. Bromont has one quad, two double chairs and three surface lifts servicing 22 runs on two mountains. Tickets are reasonable – as low as $20 – and lifts operate between 9am and 10pm Monday to Friday with an extra half hour at each end of the day at the weekends. If, within 30 minutes of purchasing your lift ticket, you are not happy with the conditions you can return the ticket and you will be given a free one for your next visit.

Much of the mountain is rated black and double black, although it is well groomed and not overwhelming for the expert skier. Nonetheless, Bromont has a 405m vertical (1,300ft). There is also a tube park.

Needless to say, Bromont has a ski school (☎ 514-534-2200 or ☎ 1-888-866-2200); a one-hour group lesson, rental equipment and a four-hour lift ticket cost $35. Private lessons start at $36 for one hour. A full range of lift tickets are also available; the rope-tow, which is open on Saturdays and Sundays, is free. The nearby town is attractive and has all the necessary services. On a small hill at the base of the moun-

Bromont

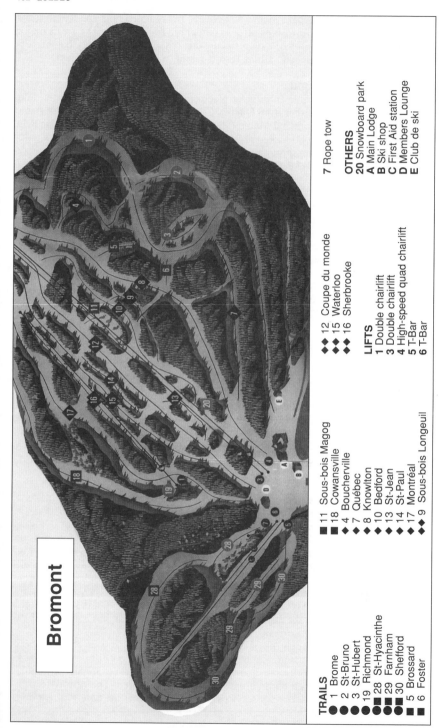

TRAILS
- ● 1 Brome
- ● 2 St-Bruno
- ● 3 St-Hubert
- ● 19 Richmond
- ■ 28 St-Hyacinthe
- ● 29 Farnham
- ■ 30 Shefford
- ■ 5 Brossard
- ■ 6 Foster

- ■ 11 Sous-bois Magog
- ■ 18 Cowansville
- ◆ 4 Boucherville
- ◆ 7 Québec
- ◆ 8 Knowlton
- ◆ 10 Bedford
- ◆ 13 St-Jean
- ◆ 14 St-Paul
- ◆ 17 Montréal
- ◆ 9 Sous-bois Longueuil

- ◆ 12 Coupe du monde
- ◆ 15 Waterloo
- ◆ 16 Sherbrooke

LIFTS
- 1 Double chairlift
- 3 Double chairlift
- 4 High-speed quad chairlift
- 5 T-Bar
- 6 T-Bar
- 7 Rope tow

OTHERS
- 20 Snowboard park
- A Main Lodge
- B Ski shop
- C First Aid station
- D Members Lounge
- E Club de ski

tain is *Château Bromont* (☎ 514-534-3433 or ☎ 1-800-304-3433) with winter rates starting from $100 inclusive.

For general information contact **Bromont Tourism Office** (☎ 514-534-2006)

MONT OWL'S HEAD

Close to the American border, just off the south-western shore of beautiful Lac Memphremagog, Mont Owl's Head is fairly isolated but is still easy to drive to being just 14 kilometres east of Mansonville. The views around Owl's Head are dramatic and with 540m (1,730ft) vertical, this medium-sized ski area has several long and enjoyable runs.

Owl's Head has one quad and six double chairs along with extensive snowmaking – despite average snowfalls which are close to 500cm (195in). Run difficulty is fairly evenly broken down with a good area for beginners. Altogether there are 27 runs.

As is true in many places, each of the resorts in The Townships has its loyal fans and despite its smaller size, Owl's Head has a large group who return consistently for the older, narrow runs and great snow. The relaxed feel of the whole area is testimony to how medium-sized resorts manage to prosper even as larger areas are constructed. Day tickets cost $30.

Owl's Head has two lodges at the base with inclusive packages starting from $55 in one lodge and $68 in the other.

For information and reservations phone ☎ 514-292-3342 or ☎ 1-800-363-3342

MONT ORFORD

Orford is an impressive resort with a good variety of skiing, located at the southern end of Mont-Orford park. The mountain is at the extreme northern end of the Appalachians and stands much on its own near the junctions of the #10 and #55 highways. The closest town, **Magog,** is situated along the northern coast of Lac Memphremagog and it has many attractive hotels and guest houses and a relaxed township night life.

The skiing at Orford happens on three peaks with four faces. Beginners will be happy skiing off Le Quatuor quad or sharing Les chaises du Nord with intermediates. The star attractions are the black, double black and yes, triple black runs. Mont Orford has an area under the triple chair with a 45-degree angle, however you may not want to fly from central BC to ski Orford's extreme zone. The triple black designation is given to expert runs which are ungroomed. There are nonetheless some great glade runs with narrow cuts and sustained steepness.

❏ MONT ORFORD
Base elevation: 310m (990ft)
Summit: 850m (2,720ft)
Vertical: 540m (1,728ft)
Lifts: 3 quads, 1 triple, 2 doubles, 2 surface
41 runs: 35% beginner, 42% intermediate, 25% advanced
Average snowfall: over 600cm (240in)
Lift operating hours: 8.30am-3.45pm

Contacts
Information and reservations: ☎ 819-843-6548 or ☎ 514-878-1411 (Montréal) or ☎ 1-800-361-6548
Snow phone: ☎ 819-843-8882 or ☎ 1-800-567-2772
Ice climbing: ☎ 1-888-475-3462
Home page: www.mt-orford.com

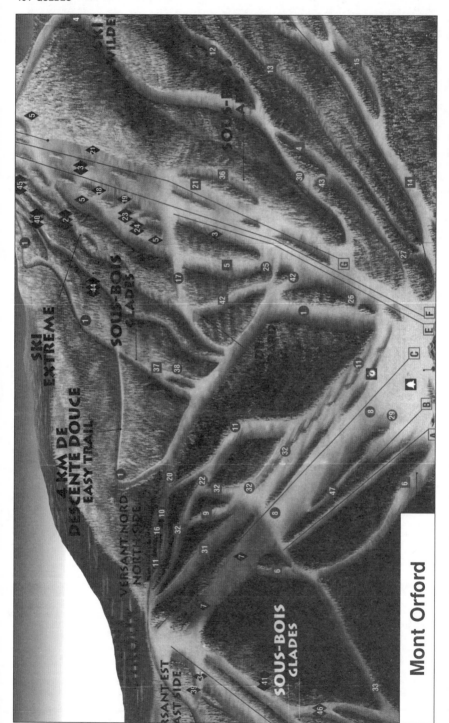

Mont Orford

MONT GIROUX (EAST SIDE)
TRAILS
● 33 Passe montagne
■ 35 Slalom
■ 34 Sherbrooke
♦ 39 Sasquatch
♦ ♦ 46 Nicolas Fontaine
♦ ♦ 41 Lloyd-Langlois

MONT GIROUX (NORTH SIDE)
TRAILS
● 8 Pente douce
● 10 Gagnon
● 11 Familiale
● 16 Petite coulée
● 20 L'Alternative
● 22 Accès
● 29 L'Initiation
● 47 Forêt magique
■ 6 Adams
■ 9 Bowen
■ 31 Tebru
■ 32 Magog
♦ 7 Magnum

MONT ORFORD
TRAILS
● 1 4 Km
● 17 Passe-partout
● 25 Connexion
● 26 Mini-passe
● 30 Inter
● 38 Boisé
● 43 Passe
■ 4 Grand Coulée
■ 36 Arcade
■ 37 Escapade
■ 42 Ballade
♦ 5 Trois-Ruisseaux
♦ 18 L'Entre-deux
♦ 19 Diversion
♦ 21 Maxi
♦ 3 Super
♦ 23 Rocher jumeaux
♦ 24 Express
♦ 2 Contour
♦ 40 Petit Canyon
♦ 44 Passe de l'ours
♦ 45 L'Intrépide

MONT DESROCHERS
TRAILS
● 12 Toussiski
● 27 Le lien
■ 13 Cascade
■ 14 Grande Allée
■ 15 Ookpic
■ 28 Descente

LIFTS
A T-Bar
B Rope tow
C Quad chairlift
D Quad chairlift
E Double chairlift
F Double chairlift
G Triple chairlift
H Quad chairlift

Orford is also a popular mountain with free-style skiers; although Whistler is steadily attracting 'the Canadian Airforce', many of Canada's top free-stylers come from Québec.

Snowboarding
With high relative snowfalls and a park off the Mi-Orford chair, this is a popular spot with boarders. The other appeal is of course the steep glades which hold their snow better – even at 45 degrees.

Cross country
The park of Mont Orford has 12 track-set trails covering 56km. The beautiful surroundings and proximity to Montréal make this a popular spot. Adult day tickets cost $8.50.

Lessons and rentals
Private lessons don't break the bank at $30 per hour, or just over $20 in a group. Orford also has a wide variety of courses for people of all ages and abilities.

A day's equipment rental goes for $23, or $15 for those eligible for the reduced rate.

Tubing can be worth a try for $11 for half a day. It is also possible to try **ice climbing** for $55 (for information and reservations phone ☎ 1-888-475-3462).

Lift tickets
	Adult	Youth/Student (14-23)	Child (6-13)
Full day	$29.35	$23.25	$17.80

If you are over 70, or 5 and under, you can ski free. Multi-day passes further reduce the cost of these already reasonable prices; a four-day pass costs $100 for an adult and $80 for a child.

Orford also has a unique system of giving credit for hours not skied.

Getting there and around
Mont Orford is just north of the #10 highway and is visible from the route. Sherbrooke is only 20 minutes away, Montréal one hour, and Québec two and a half.

Accommodation and après ski
There is a small village at the base of the mountain with several condo choices and over 2,000 beds within seven kilometres. The village accommodation is good and quite affordable, particularly when buying several day packages.

Most accommodation providers in Magog offer mountain packages with transportation. Magog is a pleasant base from where to ski the Townships and evenings in the town are enjoyable with the many cafés and pubs.

Le Village Orford (☎ 819-847-2662 or ☎ 1-800-567-7315) has full-week ski deals from $218 per person. You can also ring these numbers for information on the different on-hill condos.

Manoir Des Sables (☎ 819-847-4747 or ☎ 1-800-567-3514) has inclusive B&B deals from $87 per person. *Auberge Estrimont* (☎ 819-843-1616 or ☎ 1-800-567-7320) has packages from $70.

The region also has the *Auberge La Grande Fugue* Youth Hostel (☎ 819-843-8595) with beds for $18.

MONT SUTTON

Just north of the Vermont border and adjacent to the attractive colonial town of Sutton, Mont Sutton is the largest ski area in the Townships. The development of the area began in 1960 and it's well designed with an emphasis on glades. Snow conditions are good and hi-tech snowmaking means the whole mountain can be covered. The entire mountain face is accessed by a good lift system – most of the lifts go all the way from the bottom to the top of the mountain.

The nearby town (Sutton) epitomises the Townships and is worth a visit for its attractive Victorian architecture and a cultural feel which combines a British loyalist town with modern French Canadian culture.

It is easy to decide where you should ski at Sutton as the mountain does a very good job in keeping skiers of different abilities apart. The main base parking area accesses the one detachable quad which is the domain of intermediate skiers and has the longest vertical. Ski to the right if you are into the greens and go left, or drive up to the other parking lot, if you like blacks or double blacks. The whole advanced area has four lifts and a great variety of tree cut routes. Fortunately it's very hard to get lost, but one should be good and awake when skiing this many trees.

Snowboarding

Sutton welcomes boarders but takes an interesting position on its terrain. The management has chosen not to build a park because of the diversity offered in the glades. This is a fair decision although it's hard to believe there won't be a half-pipe one day.

Cross country

The greater Sutton area has many different trails though they are not operated by the resort.

Lessons and rentals

Ski rentals start from $17 per day; prices increase based on quality. Boards are $25 ($35 when longer than 135cm). First-time packages including a lesson and lift ticket cost $30, and $40 for boards. These must be booked in advance; contact the Ski School ☎ 514-538-1310. A wider variety of ski week deals are available.

Lift tickets

	Adult	Youth (6-17)
Full day	$39	$27

Seniors aged 65 and over and children aged 5 and under ski free. Skiing is also avail-

---

❑ MONT SUTTON

Base elevation: 400m (1,280ft)
Summit: 860m (2,750ft)
Vertical: 460m (1,472ft)
Lifts: 3 quads (1 detachable), 6 doubles
53 runs: 32% beginner, 28% intermediate, 40% advanced – much of which is considered expert glade skiing.
Average snowfall: 480cm (188in)
Lift operating hours: 8.30am-4pm

Contacts
Further information: ☎ 514-538-2545
Sutton Tourist Information: ☎ 1-800-565-8455
24hr snow phone: ☎ 514-866-7639
Ski School: ☎ 514-538-1310
Home page: www.mt-sutton.com

Mont Sutton

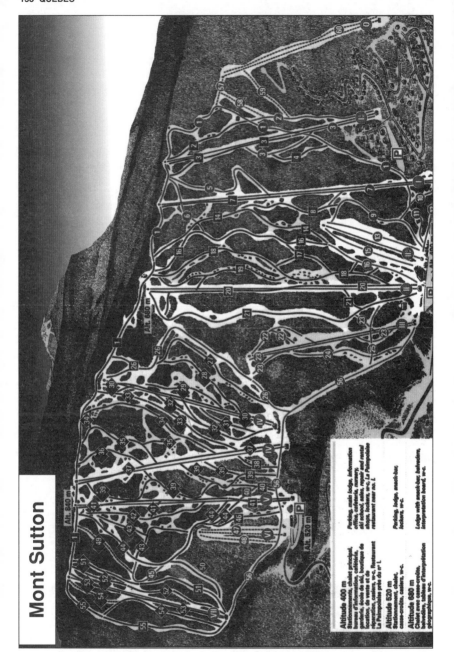

TRAILS

● 5 Loup de Loup
● 6 Bee-Bop
● 9 Yum-Yum
● 10 Connection
● 11 Passeport
● 12 Transit
● 13 Cendrillon
● 15 Cascade
● 22 Détour
● 23 ABC
● 24 Barcarole
● 25 Dou-de-Lom
● 45 Relais
● 47 *Future*
● 48 *Future*
● 56 Accès
● 57 *Future*
● 58 *Future*
● 59 *Future*
● 60 *Future*
■ 1 Alleghanys
■ 2 Coucou
■ 3 Starlet
■ 7 St-Bernard

●■ 16 Alouette
●■ 26 Youppe-Youppe
●■ 4 Sous-bois Starlet
■ 8 Ricochet
■ 14 Capucine
■ 17 Traverse
■ 18 Sous-bois II
■ 19 Caprice
■ 20 Sutton-1k
■ 21 Mohawk
■ 38 Alibi
■ 39 Sous-bois V
■ 40 Zig-Zag
■ 41 Alpine
■ 46 Sous-bois Miracle
◆ 51 Attraction
◆ 55 Exil
◆ 27 Sous-bois Youp
◆ 31 Mic-Mac
◆ 34 Surprise
◆ 35 Sous-bois IV B
◆ 37 Dynamique
◆ 42 Escapade
◆ 43 Iroquois
◆ 44 Miracle

◆ 50 Sélection
◆ 28 Challenge
◆ 29 Sous-bois Poma
◆ 30 Bo-Réal
◆ 32 Stade de slalom
◆ 36 Sous-bois IV A
◆ 49 *Future*
◆ 33 Kangarou
◆ 52 Emotion
◆ 53 Intrépide
◆ 54 Bou-bou

LIFTS

I **o-w** Double chairlift
I Double chairlift
II **o-w** Double chairlift
III Double chairlift
IV **o-w** Double chairlift
V Double chairlift
IV Quad chairlift
VII Quad chairlift
II Detachable quad chairlift

able by the hour; adults (18-64) pay $16 for the first hour and $6 for each additional hour, children (6-17) pay $14 for the first hour and $3 for each additional hour. On arrival you have to pay for the remaining hours (until closing time), at the end of your ski day you will be reimbursed for any unused hours.

Getting there and around

Sutton is 1³/₄ hours south from Montréal near the junction of routes #139 and #215. It is just over one hour from Sherbrooke and only 40 minutes from Jay, Vermont. The mountain is just a few kilometres from town.

Accommodation and après ski

There are a few rooms right on the hill and many more in Sutton itself. Prices are generally quite reasonable and many hotels open on to good cross-country and snow-shoeing areas.

The reservations office (☎ 514-663-0214 or ☎ 1-800-663-2646) will give information on condos as well as B&Bs and hotels and will make bookings. Typical on-mountain units cost between $200 and $300. The only on-hill hotel is *Paimpolaise Inn* (☎ 514-538-3213 or ☎ 1-800-263-3213) with inclusive breakfast/dinner packages from $87. B&Bs dot the landscape and generally cost around $60 for a double.

The mountain has four sheltered areas, each with a snack bar or cafeteria and a bagged après ski meal can be booked from the main lodge. The town of Sutton is perfect for strolling and visiting the quiet cafés and bistros.

Other skiing in Québec

Given the love of winter sports in Québec it is easy to assume there are downhill centres outside of the three main regions discussed. In fact most regions of Québec offer some sort of alpine fun and generally good snowfalls make skiing anywhere in Québec worthwhile.

The following can only be seen as a general guide. Most of the resorts are small regional destinations; further information can be obtained directly, or from the regional tourist boards.

Outaouais (western Québec around Hull/Ottawa)

For information and reservations phone the Regional Tourist Board ☎ 819-778-2222 or ☎ 1-800-265-7822

Mont Sainte-Marie (☎ 819-467-5200 or ☎ 1-800-567-1256) is the largest ski resort in this area and a popular spot for skiers from Canada's capital region. The resort boasts 20 runs and over 380m vertical (1,215ft). There are three lifts and lift tickets for adults cost around $30. Access is along route #105. **Fortune** (☎ 819-827-1717) near Old Chelsea has 14 trails and 300 metres.

Near Wakefield is **Vallée Edelweiss** (☎ 819-459-2328) with 18 runs, and **Vorlage** (☎ 819-459-2301) with 15 runs. **Mont Cascades** (☎ 819-827-0312) near Cantley has 14 runs. The **Centre Touristique du Lac-de-l'Argile** (☎ 819-766-2626) has four runs.

Monterégie (far south-east Québec)

For information and reservations phone the Regional Tourist Board (☎ 514-674-5555). There are a few alpine runs in this fairly flat region near **Rigaud** (☎ 514-451-5316), and at **Mont-Saint-Bruno** (☎ 514-653-3441) near Saint-Bruno-de-Montarville.

Bas-Saint-Laurent (south of Québec City)

This region has 14 trails near **Saint-Mathieu** (☎ 418-738-2299). **Parc du Mont-Comi** (☎ 418-739-4858) near Saint-Donat has four lifts, 22 runs, a snowboard park and 306 vertical metres! Adult lift tickets cost $22.

Charlevoix (east of Québec)

Le Massif with the highest vertical in Québec has been covered under the Québec City section. The **Parc regional du Mont Grand-Fonds** (☎ 418-632-5205) has 13 runs and 335 vertical metres.

Côte-Nord (north-west coast of the St Lawrence)

This huge region has skiing on **Mont Ti-Basse** (☎ 418-296-8311) near Baie-Comeau, and 23 runs near Sept-Iles at the **Station de ski Gallix** (☎ 418-766-5900).

Sanguenay-Lac-Saint-Jean (north of Québec City)

This beautiful and very independent region has a good selection of skiing with **450m vertical (1440ft)** at **Mont-Edouard** (☎ 418-272-2927) along route #170. The resort has 22 runs; tickets cost $25. **Le Valinouet** (☎ 418-673-6455 or ☎ 1-800-260-8254) near Saint-David-de-Falardeau has **350m vertical (1120ft)** serving 24 runs.

Hebertville has 15 runs on **Mont-Lac-Vert** (☎ 418-344-4000), and there are 11 runs near **Jonquière** (☎ 418-697-5090). **Alma** has five runs (☎ 418-668-3473), and **La Baie** has nine (☎ 418-687-5090). There are also some runs near Saint-Felicien and Saint-Ambroise.

PART 7: ATLANTIC CANADA

Canada's east coast provinces are probably the most relaxed in the country and although quite small in area are surprisingly diverse both culturally and physically. Prince Edward Island (PEI), which is now attached to Canada via Confederation Bridge, is a rolling island with a small, friendly population and variable snow.

New Brunswick, with nearly one million people, is shared between the Acadian French and English New Brunswickers. The province has the highest snowfall of the region and has been known to have the odd news-making dump. Like Nova Scotia beside it, New Brunswick has a significant amount of park area and lots of winter activities. Each province has variable skiing and young people now have to wear helmets in PEI.

Perhaps the wildcard skiing area in Canada is Newfoundland with at least one resort, **Marble Mountain**, worth travelling some distance to visit. Newfoundland and Labrador (NFLD) was the last province to join the Confederation having remained semi-independent until 1949. Often the publicity surrounding this province and particularly 'The Rock' of Newfoundland has to do with fishing and unemployment, but perhaps as a result of the hard economic times NFLD is making great efforts with regard to tourism. Certainly the island is ever more popular as a summer destination and the rugged scenery and wild coastline is even more dramatic in winter.

The capital, **St John's**, is North America's oldest city with a look and feel unique to the continent. As the country's wettest and foggiest city, sunscreen need not be a high priority. Labrador is the mainland component of the province and offers some of Canada's most remote skiing.

Prince Edward Island (PEI)

Canada's smallest province in both area and population has a small ski area in **Brookvale Provincial Park** (☎ 902-658-2925) with fewer than 100 vertical metres. Over 300cm of snow falls each year covering 10 runs and another five cross-country trails.

Contact
PEI Tourist Information
PO Box 940
Charlottetown C1A 7M5
☎ 902-368-4444 or ☎ 1-800-463-4734

New Brunswick

Canada's truly bilingual province has four ski areas, good snow accumulations and the second highest vertical in the Maritimes. **Crabbe Mountain** (Nova Scotia ☎ 902-895-9281), 56 kilometres from Fredericton has one chair and three surface lifts servicing

15 trails. Crabbe has a 260m vertical drop and receives over 300cm of snow annually.

Francophone Edmundston has 17 runs on **Mont Farlagne** (☎ 506-735-8401 or ☎ 506-735-6617). There are two chairs, two surface lifts and a tube slide.

Sugarloaf (☎ 506-789-2366), near Campbellton, has four lifts, eight runs and 155m vertical. **Poley Mountain** (☎ 506-433-2201) has just over 200m vertical, 15 trails and a half-pipe. Poley has a quad and three surface lifts.

There are many other popular areas in New Brunswick for cross-country and snowmobiling.

Contact
New Brunswick Tourist Information
PO Box 12345,
Fredericton, E3B 5C3
☎ 506-444-4081 or ☎ 1-800-561-0123

Nova Scotia

Close to Ingonish Beach in the bilingual north of the most populated province in Atlantic Canada, **Cape Smokey** (☎ 902-285-2778 or ☎ 1-800-564-2040) has 13 runs descending 310 metres right to the Atlantic ocean! There are two lifts and some heavy snow. There are also some very good cross-country trails through **Cape Breton Highlands National Park**. Also on Cape Breton is **Ben Eoin** (☎ 902-828-2222) with 10 runs, just west of Sydney.

Near Antigonish, **Keppoch** (☎ 902-863-2271) has two lifts and claims two triple blacks. **Ski Martock** (☎ 902-798-9501), 10 kilometres west of Windsor, has seven runs and eight lifts! **Wentworth** (☎ 902-548-2089) is 50 kilometres from Truro and has four lifts and 250 vertical metres serving 21 runs. Wentworth also has several kilometres of cross-country trails.

Contact
Nova Scotia Tourist Information
PO Box 456
Halifax, B3J 2R5
☎ 982-425-5781 or ☎ 1-800-565-0000

Newfoundland and Labrador

Travelling to the Rock (Newfoundland) in winter involves a boat from North Sydney, Nova Scotia to Port aux Basques on the south-west of the island. Boat routes to St John's do not operate during the winter months and should you wish to sail to Labrador over winter you'll need an ice breaker. Services are operated by **Marine Atlantic** (☎ 1-800-341-7981), reservations are advised.

Labrador City has skiing on **Smokey Mountain** (☎ 709-944-3505) with four lifts and 300m vertical. Should you fly all the way to Labrador City, why not call in at **Goose Bay** (☎ 709-896-8162) for a few runs en route.

The Rock has a few minor ski clubs along with 15 runs near Clarenville on **White Hills** (☎ 709-466-7773). **Copper Creek Mountain** (☎ 709-532-4338) is NFLD's newest resort and has seven runs looking out on beautiful views over Baie Verte.

It is always worth taking cross-country skis to NFLD as there are many great parks worth exploring.

Contact
Newfoundland & Labrador Provincial Tourism Office
PO Box 8730
St John's
NF - AIB 4K2
☎ 709-729-2831 or 1-800-563-6353
email: info@tourism.gov.nf.ca
home page: www.gov.nf.ca/tourism

MARBLE MOUNTAIN
One of the most highly rated mountains in eastern Canada, Marble has all the trimmings of a good resort. An hour's flight from St John's, Marble is just minutes away from Newfoundland's second largest city, **Corner Brooke**. Along with the good skiing and beautiful views, Newfoundland is a unique place for a vacation with a cultural identity of its own.

While Marble's area is not huge, runs are well planned and the vertical is high enough to make the skiing enjoyable and your legs tired. The high snowfalls provide Marble with some heavy ocean powder. There is one long beginner run so everyone can enjoy the views, and some good challenging advanced terrain.

Marble has a snowboard park off to the side and all sorts of cross-country and snowmobiling tracks. Needless to say the resort is getting lots of 'Newfies' on to skis with the variety of lessons and the affordability of the rental equipment. For information and reservations phone ☎ 709-637-7600.

Getting there and around
If you're not a Newfoundlander, Marble is a bit of a trek – but the effort is worth making for easterners and indeed all Canadians because it means visiting our most distinct province. Bringing the car always means a six-hour boat ride, but it is great to have a vehicle to explore the area. From Port aux Basques, Corner Brooke in an easy drive north. Flying to Deer Lake is an easy option. **Break Away Vacations** (☎ 1-800-976-2725) organises trips, as does **Maxxim Vacations** (☎ 1-800-567-6666).

Accommodation and après ski
The village around Marble Mountain is expanding and there is a beautiful new lodge at the base with restaurants serving some Newfoundland specialities and, of course, a pub. *Foothill Cabins* (☎ 709-634-4879) has rooms for as low as $60 (plus large quantities of NFLD tax). *Marble Mountain Cabins* (☎ 709-634-2237) start as low as $50 (plus taxes).

Contact NFLD Tourism for a list of rooms. Corner Brooke has a good selection of affordable hotels and motels as well as lively Newfie bars.

❏ MARBLE MOUNTAIN
Base elevation: 50m (160ft)
Summit: 540m (1,728ft)
Vertical: 490m (1,570ft)
Lifts: 3 quads and 2 surface
27 runs: 4 beginner, 11 intermediate, 12 advanced
Average snowfall: 500cm (16ft)

GLOSSARY

GLOSSARY FOR SKIERS IN FRENCH CANADA

As many Canadians are aware the French spoken in the Great White North can be somewhat different to that in France, which means that not all terms can be used in both countries. For those who do speak the language the French way, you will rarely have difficulty making yourselves understood, while the response may not be quite so clear.

As is true with most languages, Canadian French varies significantly from region to region, and French speaking visitors will enjoy hearing the different accents. The staff in the vast majority of ski areas are bilingual although signs are not always in both languages, particularly on some of the smaller more remote hills. The bigger issue in Québec is the fact that road signs are only in French. Fortunately for Anglophones it is never too difficult to find someone who speaks some English.

Basic French terms and phrases

Do you speak English?	*Parlez-vous Anglais?*
Hello (Good Day)	*Bonjour*
Good evening	*Bonsoir*
Goodbye	*Au revoir*
Yes	*Oui*
No	*Non*
Please	*S'il vous plaît*
Thank you	*Merci*
Where is the…?	*Où est le/la…?*

Skiing terms

Mountain	*Mont*
Snow	*Neige*
Downhill skiing	*Ski alpine*
Cross country	*Ski de font*
Classic stride style	*Pas alternatif*
Skating stride style	*Pas patin*
Snowboard	*Planche à neige*
Snowboarding	*Surf des neiges*
Snowboard park	*Parc de planches à neige*
Half-pipe	*Demi-lune*
Ski resort/area	*Centre/Station de ski*
Ski school	*Ecole de ski*
Repair	*Réparation*
Rentals	*Location*
Trails	*Pistes*
Glades/treed areas	*Sous-bois*
Moguls	*Bosses*
Easy (green)	*Facile*
Difficult/advanced (blue)	*Difficile*
Very difficult (black)	*Très difficile*
Extremely difficult (double black)	*Extrêmement difficile*
Caution	*Attention*

Skiing terms (cont)

Slow skiing zone	*Zone à vitesse reduite*
Easiest route down	*Chemin le plus facile*
Lift tickets	*Billetterie*
Lifts	*Remontées*
Chairlift	*Télésiège*
Detachable chairlift	*Télésiège debrayable*
First aid	*Clinique*
Patrol	*Patrouille*
Shuttle	*Navette*

Glossary for non-skiers

Alpine skiing	Downhill skiing.
Back-country skiing	Winter trekking using skis.
Biathlon	An Olympic event in which cross-country skiing is combined with target shooting.
Black (runs)	Advanced (double and triple black runs are for experts; triple black runs are rare and don't generally warrant the designation).
Blue (runs)	Intermediate runs.
Bunny slopes	Very easy beginner runs.
Classic-style	The traditional form of cross-country skiing.
Clinic	A lesson in which the teaching is focussed on one aspect of the sport, such as bumps, turns, powder etc.
Cross-country skiing	Cross-country skis are generally thinner and more flexible than alpine skis and the skiers' heel is not bound to the ski. Cross-country skiing is a traditional form of winter travel and it is done on groomed tracks and untouched snow.
Detachable quad	A high speed, four-person chair lift which detaches from the main rope in order to slow down for people to get on and off.
Double	A chair lift for two people at a time.
Gates	Plastic posts or markers that racers must stay within on a course. Whether the gates are for slalom or giant slalom is decided by the distance between the gates and the number of turns required.
Green (runs)	The easiest run for beginners.
Groomed trails	Runs/trails where the snow has been flattened and spread out by machines. Grooming is particularly important when snow-making is used.
Half-pipe	A hollowed area of snow which resembles half a pipe and which is mostly used by snowboarders.
Heli-skiing	The ultimate (and most expensive) way to alpine ski. Helicopters are used to transport skiers high in to the mountain to find the best, untouched snow. Usually geared towards experienced skiers, heli-ski packages cost hundreds of dollars.

Luge	An Olympic event in which one or two people ride a stylised sled at speeds exceeding 100km/h down a track.
Moguls	Naturally occurring snowy bumps that form on ungroomed runs. Generally these are left to form on steeper runs and are popular with more advanced skiers and those who have strong knees.
Nordic skiing	Cross-country and non-alpine skiing.
Parabolic skis	A new style of shaped ski which seems to aid turning. Parabolics are popular with new skiers and with many fans of powder skiing.
Poling	Having to push with your ski poles because the ground is flat.
Quad	A four-seater chair lift.
Rope tow	One of the earliest kinds of lift; skiers hang on to a rope to be pulled uphill. These are still common on beginner slopes.
Skating style	The modern style of cross-country skiing where skiers look as if they are skating; the style looks awkward but it is efficient.
Ski chutes	Narrow steep runs which are generally found between large out-crops of rock.
Ski fields	Ski slopes.
Ski in/Ski out	Accommodation where you can literally ski to the door.
Ski-joring	An unusual sport of Norwegian origin which involves a cross-country skier being pulled by one to three dogs – traditionally huskies.
Ski touring	Back-country ski trips – there are many government-administered huts in undeveloped areas where back-country skiers can stay.
Snow-cat skiing	A snow cat is a vehicle with treads that can climb slopes to drop skiers off on different skiing terrain. It is more expensive than a lift ticket but less than a heli-skiing trip.
Snow guns	Machines used for making snow.
Snow-shoes	Racket-shaped frames which are strapped onto footwear in order to avoid sinking in deep snow.
Surface lift	Any ski lift in which the skier is pulled uphill with their skis still on the ground.
Telemarking	The traditional style of skiing where one's heels are not clamped on to the ski.
Tow rope	(see Rope tow).
T-bar	A two-person surface lift which is shaped like an upside down 'T'.
Track-set trails	Cross-country trails in which a machine is used to cut tracks for classic-style skiing and for all styles when going downhill.
Treed slope	A tree-covered slope.
Triple	A three-seater chair lift.
Tubing	Descending or tobogganing downhill on large, inflated inner-tubes.

Glossary for non-Canadians

Bagged meal	Packed lunch.
Interact	Paying for goods or services directly with a bank (a debit not a credit) card.
Lounge	A kind of pub/restaurant with table service and a relaxed atmosphere.
RV park	An area where recreational vehicles (RVs) or motor homes can hook-up for power, water and sewage. Costs are often around $20 per day.
Touque	The most common and best known Canadian hat.
Unsealed road	A gravel road (ie with a loose surface).

INDEX